D1096126

10-
6-41

This booklet is one of a series prepared by the Loomis Museum Association, a non-profit distributing organization sponsored by the Naturalist Department of Lassen Volcanic National Park. The Association is dedicated to the accumulation and dissemination of information concerning the history and natural history of this park. Toward this end it has published the following books available by mail. The post office address is Mineral, California. During the summer, these publications are also available at the Loomis Museum sales desk at Manzanita Lake, Lassen Volcanic National Park.

GEOLOGY OF LASSEN'S LANDSCAPE,
     Schulz .... 55¢

PICTORIAL HISTORY OF THE LASSEN
     VOLCANO, Loomis .... 85¢

GUIDE TO LASSEN PEAK HIGHWAY,
     Schulz .... 25¢

STORIES OF LASSEN'S PLACE NAMES,
     Schulz .... 40¢

BIRDS OF LASSEN VOLCANIC NATIONAL
     PARK AND VICINITY, Stebbins .... 85¢

FISH AND FISHING IN LASSEN VOLCANIC
     NATIONAL PARK, Potts .... 40¢

INDIANS OF THE LASSEN AREA
     Schulz .... 85¢

For mail orders please add 12% for postage and packing. If the addressee is in California also add 3% sales tax. Prices are subject to change without notice.

INDIANS
OF
LASSEN
VOLCANIC NATIONAL PARK AND VICINITY

by
Paul E. Schulz

Published by the

Loomis Museum Association
Lassen Volcanic National Park
Mineral, California

Copyright
1954

Printed in the United States of America
Susanville *Lassen Litho* California

PREFACE

It is with some temerity that the author, a geologist by training and an interpretive naturalist by occupation, undertakes to compile this booklet on Indians who once inhabited the vicinity of Lassen Peak.

The main mission of a naturalist, as he functions in the National Park Service, is to act as an interpreter of technical information gathered together by research scientists. It is his obligation as well as his privilege to make these data of history and natural history available for visitors to units administered by the National Park Service of the United States Department of the Interior. The Park Naturalist is challenged to create in visitors an eager interest by presenting information in an appealing manner so that the great stories of the respective areas may be learned easily and pleasantly. In doing this, visitors gain fuller understanding and hence better appreciation of the significance of these areas. This leads to greater enjoyment of the scenic masterpieces, the scientific natural wonders, and the historic shrines of areas of the National Park System. Not only is the visitor's enjoyment enhanced by his active reception of the interpretive facilities and services offered him by the Federal Government, but his pride is stimulated in these areas which have been set aside for his own use as well as for the benefit of future generations. A citizen's pride in his park areas in turn develops a love of country. It also promotes a sense of responsibility which helps the National Park Service fight vandalism, fire carelessness, and litter carelessness to the ultimate benefit of all concerned.

Little on the pages which follow may be classed as original material for it is in the role of interpreter that the undersigned has assembled information gleaned by qualified students.

The term "Amerind" instead of the traditional word "Indian" was seriously considered for use in this book but finally rejected. Ever since Christopher Columbus' historic mistake the word Indian has had a confusing two-fold meaning. Columbus, of course, thought that he had been successful in reaching India when his little fleet touched the shores of the New World. Hence he applied the word Indian to the people he found there, supposing them to be natives of India. The term Amerind is a coined contraction of the words: American Indian. The use of Amerind has been advocated by some authors to do away with confusion, and it does seem to be an excellent name, but it has not enjoyed wide usage by the American public.

I am deeply indebted to the following named persons whose research and learned writings have provided the bulk of the information contained in the present publication. The bibliography carries the titles of the specific references used.

Dr. Roland B. Dixon	Dr. Saxton T. Pope
Mr. Thomas R. Garth	Dr. Carl O. Sauer
Dr. E. W. Gifford	Dr. Edward Sapir
Dr. Robert F. Heizer	Dr. Leslie Spier
Dr. Stanislaw Klimek	Miss Erminie W. Voegelin
Dr. A. L. Kroeber	Dr. T. T. Waterman

Properly, specific credit should be given in the text for each fact and quotation taken from the works of others, but the result would in this case have been unwieldy and of no practical benefit to the readers whom this book is intended to reach. It is hoped that professional ethnologists into whose hands this volume may fall will forgive this unorthodox usage of the research results of serious students.

Mrs. Selina La Marr (Boonookoo-ee-menorra) was a valuable and gracious informant. Thanks are due again to Dr. E. W. Gifford, Director of the Museum of Anthropology at the Univeristy of California, for many courtesies, including donation of a copy of Dixon's rare "Yana Indians" and also for his constructive perusal of the manuscript. Others who assisted the author were Mrs. Grace Schulz, Miss Lois Bell of the University of California "University Explorer" radio program, and Mr. Louis Caywood, National Park Service archeologist. Dr. J. H. Woolsey, M.D., earned gratitude of the author by donation of his personal copy of Pope's "Medical History of Ishi". Miss Lilian Nisbet of the Tehama County Library was helpful in the securing of other reference materials.

Most Californians are vitally interested in the Indians of this state, yet few are aware of the excellent California State Indian Museum operated by the Division of Beaches and Parks. The Indian Museum is open to the public daily, free of charge, in a separate building on the grounds of Sutter's Fort State Historical Monument in Sacramento. The author highly commends this museum to you. It contains a wealth of authentic materials which have been organized into handsome and exciting story-telling exhibits of first quality by Curator Jack Dyson.

Paul E. Schulz
Park Naturalist
Lassen Volcanic National Park
Fall 1954

CONTENTS

Chapter I

PREHISTORIC MAN COMES TO NORTH AMERICA

Archeological studies of human remains from all over the world have shown beyond serious question that man originated in the Eastern Hemisphere about a million years ago. Meager remnants of prehistoric skeletons of man and his tools, hearths, and debris heaps have been found in deposits of late Cenozoic time, Chapter Five of earth's history. This late Cenozoic period starting about a million years ago is called the Pleistocene or Ice Age. These discoveries show the orderly processes of survival of the fittest and of evolution developing successive generations of man with refined physical and mental qualities, ultimately producing modern man.

During the Ice Age there were four separate times during which ice formation on all continents of the earth increased tremendously. Just what caused changes in climate to make this possible is not definitely known. Slight changes in amount of carbon dioxide in the air, which could have been affected by the amount of volcanic activity or by major c h a n g e s in the amount of plant life in existence, may have affected the climate. Slight variations in the orbit of the earth in its course around the sun may also have had their influence. Even today it would require a drop of only a few degrees in the average annual temperature of the earth's climate to produce a large increase in ice formation. All that is required is that a little more snow falls each winter than will melt in the summer. Thus, each year the e x c e s s would gradually build up glaciers and continental ice sheets, producing another "ice stage" in a few thousands of years.

The area of ice in the world today is relatively small: under 6 million square miles, about the same as that existing during each of the four interglacial (warm climate) stages of the Pleistocene. During the four glacial stages of the Ice Age, continental ice sheets increased their areas by three or four times, also becoming larger in size in each successive cold cycle. The latest and most extensive of these glacial times, the Wisconsin Stage, actually saw two ice advances with a brief recession separating them about 60,000 years ago.

During each glacial stage tremendous amounts of water were removed from the oceans and deposited on the continents as ice fields. This involved amounts of as much as 20 million cubic miles of water, causing world-wide lowering of sea level of about 150 or 200 feet. Today the sea b e t w e e n Alaska and Siberia is very shallow. It is not difficult to realize that lowered sea level during the glacial stages of the ice age drained the water from this and other shallow sea floors exposing these as land links or "land bridges" which extended between continents and islands. This state of affairs made possible the overland migration of man to the Western Hemisphere.

In his illuminating paper "Early Relations of Man to Plants" Sauer has pointed out that early man's migrations to the New World were not the result of mere aimless wanderings. Peking Man of the first interglacial stage about 900,000 years ago in Asia used fire in established hearths. He ate both cooked meats and vegetables. This evidence indicates at least a semi-sedentary family life. Since he had learned to make himself more comfortable generally by remaining in one favorable place, it follows logically that even primitive Peking Man migrated only when he could improve his lot by doing so. He moved on only when he was forced to do so by a failing food supply or because of crowded conditions caused by increasing numbers of his fellow men. It is believed that not only Peking Man, but his descendants were as sedentary as their food supply allowed them to be. Dr. Sauer observes that

". . . . the history of human population (numbers) is a succession of higher and higher levels, each rise to a new level being brought about by the discovery of more food either through occupation of a new territory or through increase in food producing skill."

The invention of a better tool, improved food preparation, discovery of new foods, better storage, or utilization would bring about this increase in food availability.

Apparently the twin circumstances of the need for more food and the existence of a dry land connection between Asia and North America enabled a series of migrations of prehistoric men to the New World. The migrations did not occur just during one glacial stage, nor during the last 15 or 25,000 years as some have claimed, but continued interruptedly over a period of many thousands of years. Perhaps such migrations started as long ago as 300,000 years--- whenever land connections permitted and other conditions warranted. As a result, we find a number of stocks of Old World Man at various levels of cultural development coming into the Americas. Naturally a variety of plant and animal species migrated in both directions between the Old and New Worlds of their own accord, in addition to those which might have been brought along by prehistoric man.

A classic example of plant migration to the New World is that of California's celebrated redwoods. In China just a few years ago the little changed ancestors of these trees, the still-growing Metasequoia were discovered. In rocks of the most recent era (Chapter Five of earth's history) the step by step migration of the changing redwood ancestors can be followed by studying successively younger rock layers in Siberia, Alaska, and in Canada and northwest United States. These relics and imprints of the foliage, fruits, and even of wood texture of these ancient trees were covered by sands and muds, and thus preserved in stone as fossils. This has made it possible to identify the ancestral redwood species and to demonstrate their march to California. It is interesting to note how the redwoods changed in the process, evolving by degrees to cope with new conditions of climate and soil during their slow migrations. At length today two distinct and unique Sequoias are to be found living only in California. One, the Coast Redwood, has adapted itself to coastal fogs and reproduction by sprouting root shoots. The other, restricted to drier areas of the west slope of the Sierra, the Sierra Redwood or Big Tree, has its needles reduced to small scales to withstand the drier climate, and reproduces only by seed.

Sauer observes that the stone implements of prehistoric man are the best preserved relics of his culture and are the most easily found. Unfortunately the less durable and less easily recognized relics of skin, bone, wood, and vegetable fibers which are equally or often even more important clues to the past, have been altered beyond recognition or completely destroyed. As a result these disappeared or their camouflaged remnants have been overlooked and passed unrecognized by even careful students seeking to learn the details of this fascinating story of the how's and why's and when's of your ancestors and mine in Europe and also of the Indians in Asia and in North America in general, and of those of the Lassen area in particular.

Chapter II
EARLY CULTURES IN NORTH AMERICA

The fact that skeletons of primitive forms of man have so far not been discovered in the Western Hemisphere does not mean that ancestral forms preceding modern man did not migrate to the New World in remote times. It is that erroneous idea which has caused some persons to reason that man arrived here only in the final glacial stage. Good evidence has been presented to suggest that the sites he would have been most likely to inhabit might be submerged at present or may have been especially vulnerable to destruction by erosion.

Certain primitive peoples of the New World (in South America) do no boiling of foods and do not have the dog, indicating very early immigration from the Old World. Dr. Sauer suggests a date during the third glacial stage, the Kansan, about 300,000 years ago instead of the Wisconsin Glacial Stage of 15,000 or 25,000 years ago as some have contended.

At the present level of archeological and paleontological knowledge of prehistoric man in North America, Sauer recognizes five basic early cultures. These are listed below in the order of their apparent appearances in the New World.

The most primitive and oldest culture of man recognized to date is very difficult to detect, for its evidences were of a fragile nature. Few traces of it remain to be seen today. This first culture known in North America lacks both stone weapon points and grinding stones. These items were also found lacking in the cultures of some isolated contemporary peoples of both North and South America.

The second oldest culture in North America was that of the Ancient Food Grinders which appears to have been widespread in the rather rainy climate of the Mississippi and Pacific regions of North America. These people built fireplaces or hearths---beds of collected stones. They used a grinding slab of stone on which a handstone was rubbed to crush hard seeds. This indicates a greater variety of foods than used in the earlier culture. A number of crude pounding tools such as choppers and scrapers were employed as were a few rude knives of stone. It is of interest and significance that use of the grinder and grinding slab disappeared completely from most or all of this area later. The well known metate and mano grinding devices of the Southwest were introduced much later, along with the growing of corn or maize, from the Central

American region. Coiled basketry appears to be identified with
this second culture too, such articles being essential as containers
for collection of seeds, winnowing, et cetera. Studies of the
evidence in the field show also that these peoples were sedentary
to the extent of developing refuse mounds or middens. The fact
that this culture is not found in Europe or in Asia indicates that
it developed in the Western Hemisphere.

About 35,000 years ago the third culture appears to have developed. It was one in which hunting was of major importance.
These hunters were not nomads, however, for the building of hearths,
accumulations of artifacts, and also the general use of seed grinding stones, all indicate rather sedentary habits. This culture is
characterized by the presence of dart or spear throwers, an invention of European origin. This indicates more recent migrations
from the Old World. These darts were stone tipped and propelled
with a spear thrower or atlatl, making hunting of animal food much
more effective than in the case of earlier cultures.

The fourth culture is that known by the names Folsom and Yuma.
In these people interest in plant foods and fibers was slight, for
this was primarily a mobile hunting culture. The people were not
sedentary, but moved around.

Well after the disappearance of the glaciers of the Ice Age, late
comers from the Old World brought a fifth culture to the Americas.
These people used the bow and arrow with its small and finely
worked stone point. Fish hooks were used and many stone implements were well polished. This too is the first culture of the New
World with which the dog was associated.

In Eastern North America, and particularly well known in the
Southwest, are abundant archeological evidences from easily recognized prehistoric living sites. These reveal a succession of more
recent cultures and changes within cultures, as well as movement
of early peoples. In contrast there are relatively few recognized
prehistoric sites in California which tell much about early customs
and material culture of aboriginal man. Some productive areas
which have been found are notably the following: The Farmington
Resevoir area of Stanislaus County more than 4,000 years old ---
possibly much older, Kingsley Cave, the Santa Barbara area, and
the off-shore islands to the southwest of it. There are also a few
shell mounds in the Los Angeles--Ventura area and more numerous
and extensive ones in the San Francisco Bay vicinity. Of the latter
shell mounds A. L. Kroeber writes:

    ". . . . all the classes of objects (shells, refuse, mortars,
    pestles, obsidian, charmstones, and bone awls) in question

AREAS AND SUBAREAS OF CULTURES
IN AND ABOUT CALIFORNIA
after A. L. Kroeber

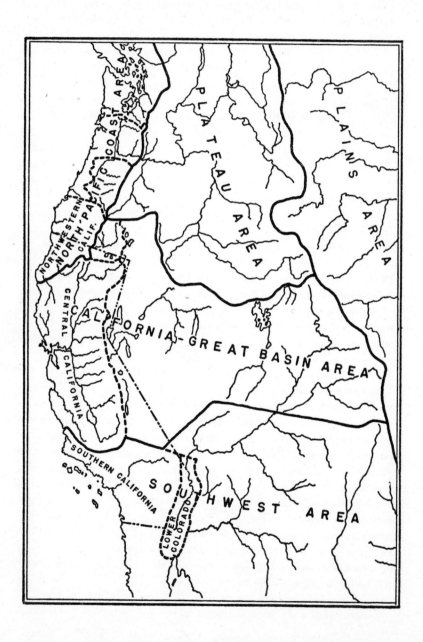

occur at the bottom, middle, and top of the mounds, and . . . .
they occur with substantially the same frequency. In other
words, the natives of the San Francisco region traded the same
materials from the same localities one, two, or three thousand
years ago as when they were d i s c o v e r e d at the end of the
eighteenth century. They ate the same food, in nearly the
same proportions (only mammalian bones became more abundant
in higher levels), prepared it in substantially the same manner,
and sewed skins, rush mats, and coiled baskets similarly to
their recent descendants. Even their religion was conserva-
tive, since the identical charms seem to have been regarded
potent. In a word, the basis of culture remained identical
during the whole of the shell-mound period.

"When it is remembered that . . . . the beginning of this
period (occurred) more than 3,000 years ago, it is clear that
we are here confronted by a historical fact of extraordinary
importance. It means that at the time when Troy was besieged
and Solomon was building the temple, at a period when even
Greek civilization had not yet taken on the traits that we regard as characteristic, when only a few scattering foundations
of specific modern culture were being laid and our own northern ancestors dwelled in unmitigated barbarism, the native
Californian already lived in all essentials like his descendant
of today. In Europe and Asia, change succeeded change of the
profoundest type. On this far shore of the Pacific, civilization,
such as it was, remained immutable in all fundamentals.

". . . . The permanence of Californian culture . . . . is of
far more than local interest. It is a fact of significance in the
history of civilization."
Successive intrusions of different peoples and the isolation of
the resultant developing Indian tribes, century after century, gave
rise to many diverse languages. Although some were mere dialects,
there were about 750 different North American Indian languages.

Chapter III

THE CALIFORNIA INDIANS

Dr. A. L. Kroeber's map shows all tribes within the present political boundaries of the State of California. The tribes of the extreme northwest corner and those of the southern tip of the state are not typical of what we generally think of as "California Indians".

Although it may not be scientifically sound to do so, it is often convenient to refer to the Indian tribes of the California region collectively. The term "Digger Indians" is frequently used for this purpose with a somewhat disparaging connotation. The origin of this name is traceable to white traders and pioneers who observed that local Indians dug extensively for a number of food items, hence the name Digger was applied. However, this is a poor name as digging was but one of many methods the Indians used to secure food. Besides, digging was by no means peculiar to Indians of the California area. It is best, therefore, simply to use the term California Indians, if one wishes to refer to this group of tribes as a whole.

In connection with the nickname Digger Indian, it is of interest to note that the California tribes used the conspicuous pine of the foothills, *Pinus sabiniana,* as a source of edible pine nuts and for other purposes too. Because the so called Digger Indians used these trees so much, the pioneers named the conifers Digger Pines, a name recognized today as the proper common name of that tree.

California tribes are usually not considered high culturally among Indians generally, yet Yurok, Pomo, and Chumash are equal to any tribe in North America in wood, bone, steatite, obsidian, feather, and skin work, while local tribes of the Lassen area made basketry of a variety and quality unsurpassed elsewhere.

Although there were local differences in food habits, the California Indians as a group had a highly diversified diet in contrast to the so—called one—food tribes in surrounding areas. Of course it is an over—simplification to speak of one—food tribes, for all ate quite a variety of foods. Yet, it is true that several cultures had been built upon the great abundance and importance of one particular food item as compared to all other foods eaten. North of California, Indians built their culture largely upon the salmon. To the east were tribes which depended upon the bison for most of their needs, and southeast of California the Southwest Indians built their culture around the all important maize or native corn.

INDIAN TRIBAL DISTRIBUTION
IN NORTHERN CALIFORNIA
after A. L. Kroeber

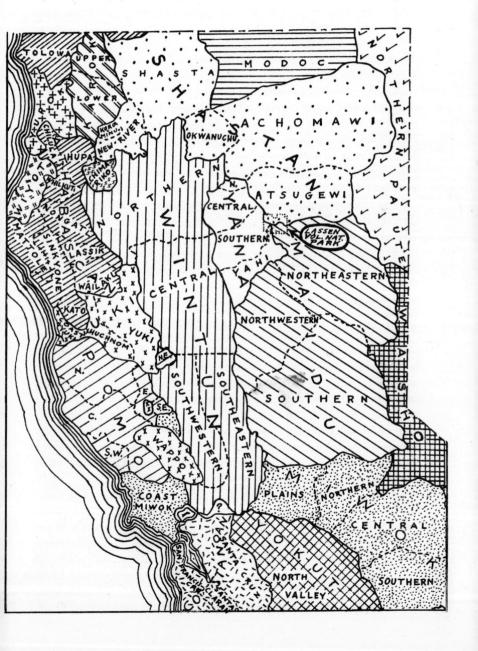

In any of these regional groups, if the main food item failed, disaster struck the tribes. In contrast, the Californians, with diversified eating habits, had four major food sources: fish, game, roots, and seeds or nuts. Each was important and the failure of any one caused hardship, but by no means the serious disaster which befell the more specialized groups of Indians if their main food supply item failed. If any one item of the California Indian diet were to be selected as the most important and universal food, one of the nuts, the acorn would have to be named.

California Indians are often regarded to have been lazy and shiftless. To be sure there were such individuals, but we have that type of person in our midst too, and I dare say in equal or greater percentage. As a matter of fact, Indians generally could not afford to be lazy---there was no beneficent government to coddle them. It was largely a case of sink or swim. They had to provide their own shelter, food, and clothing as well as what amusement and extras---hardly to be called luxuries---they wished to enjoy. These things were all wrought from the wilderness with their own bare hands, using only wood, stone, and fire as tools. These native Americans lived in a stone-age culture. Metals, the wheel, domesticated herd animals, and agriculture were unknown to California Indians. Although there was some seasonal migration, there were no truly nomadic or wandering tribes in California.

In California there were 103 separate tribes each speaking its own language. To be sure, some were mere dialects of others, but there were 21 tongues completely distinct from each other and mutually unintelligible. These belonged to several unrelated language families, as shown on the second map.

As suggested above, Kroeber has shown that we are technically incorrect in referring to the California Indians as a single group of tribes. Within the political boundaries of the State of California there were actually three separate cultures with a number of subcultures, which were as follows: The small area in the northwest corner of the state, the Klamath River drainage, was occupied by the Northwest California Sub-culture, a part of the North Pacific Coast Culture which extended into British Columbia. The California-Great Basin Culture had three representatives in the state: the smallest or Lutuami Sub-culture, represented by the Modoc tribe only, extended down from the north across the east central portion of the northern boundary of California. The next larger was the Great Basin Sub-culture just east of the Cascade-Sierra backbone. The third and largest sub-culture of the California-Great Basin Culture was that of the Central California tribes (the Diggers

INDIAN LANGUAGE GROUPS OF NORTHERN CALIFORNIA
and the families to which they belong, after A. L. Kroeber

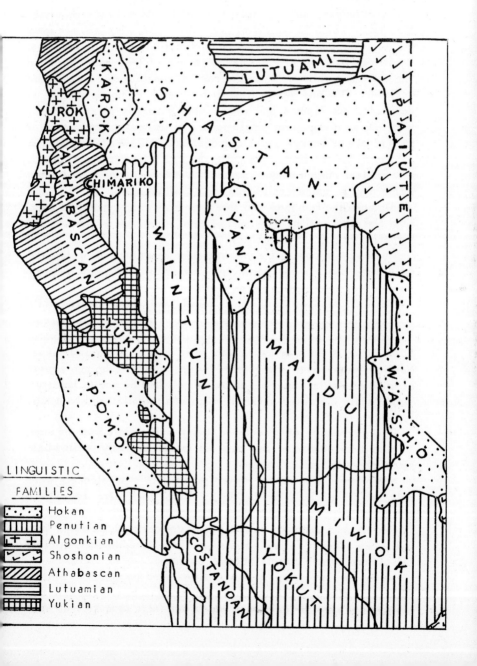

of the pioneer), extending westward from the Cascade-Sierra crest to the Pacific Ocean across the bulk of the state. The fifth subculture is known as the Southern California comprising the area south of the Tehachapi Mountains from the coast east across the Colorado River, being a part of the Southwest Culture.

Nevertheless, some generalities hold, and at the risk of the inaccuracy which is typical of generalizations, we might set forth the following customs as being characteristic of California Indians:

Animal flesh bulked a smaller volume of food eaten than did vegetable materials---or, in the case of coastal peoples, than did seafoods. Dog and reptile flesh were considered poisonous or undesirable, but insects and worms were generally eaten. Acorns were the most important single food. All tribes utilized seeds of such plants as buckeye, grass, sedge, and sunflower family plants. All items, but the first, were collected with a basketry seed beater in a conical burden basket, parched, winnowed, ground, and eaten either dry, as unleavened bread, or as boiled mush.

Although the fish hook and line were known throughout the area, most fishing was done by means of nets, weirs, use of poison, and harpoons thrust, but not thrown.

Hunting with bow and arrow was most important. Disguise and dogs were used in the north, but surrounding the game was the common means of hunting in the south.

The northern bow was short, broad, and sinew backed while southern Californians used long narrow bows without reinforcement.

Arrows were usually two-piece and tipped with obsidian points. Three different arrow releases were used among California Indians. Northern arrows were straightened by use of a hole through a piece of wood or similar material, and were polished by use of horsetail stalks while a grooved squarish soapstone (steatite) did both jobs in the south.

Basketry was highly developed, being California's best art form. The northern quarter of the area did twined basketry; coiled basketry prevailed elsewhere.

Cloth was unknown, but woven rabbit skin strip blankets were universal, especially for bedding. Rush mats were twined and sewn.

Pottery was unknown except for a very crude undecorated form in the San Joaquin Valley, an intrusion from the Southern California Sub-culture where pottery became important.

Music of California was characterized by singing, rattles, whistles, split slap sticks, flute, and musical bow. The last two instruments were the only ones which were able to make real melodies, but amazingly, neither one was used for dances or ceremonies. California Indians were virtually without any drums--- the exception being a single headed flat foot drum used in ceremonial sweathouse chambers of the tribes in the Sacramento and San Joaquin Valleys.

Dress of California women was a front and a back apron of skin --- especially buckskin --- or of plant fiber. Men wore nothing or a folded skin about the hips or between the legs. In bad weather both sexes used cape - like or wrap - around (over one arm and under the other) skin robes. In localized areas the brimless dome - shaped basketry cap was worn by women. Hair of both sexes was long (but shorn in mourning) and frequently put up in nets by men. Men removed their beards by pulling with their fingers.

In mountain areas social and religious cults were lacking. In the extreme northwest corner wealth dances were held; in central California the secret society and Kuksu dances, in the south the Jimsonweed initiation system, and in the Colorado River area the dreamsong ceremony flourished.

Houses varied from open enclosures and brush or bark shelters to frame structures more or less completely dug into the ground and covered with bark, brush, and dirt, usually with a roof entrance and or one to the south; this was the earth lodge. In the extreme northwest housing was not the earth lodge, but a structure built on top of the ground; hand- split planks were used in its construction.

Sweat houses were of the earth lodge type, often of daily service and in northern areas, lived in too. Sweat houses of California were not heated by steam, but directly with fire.

Boats generally were of rushes tied into balsa rafts or into boat shapes. In addition one- piece dugout canoes from tree logs were typical of the northern portion of California, becoming progressively more refined in workmanship and in design to the northwest. A unique lashed split board canoe was made by channel island tribes in the Santa Barbara vicinity.

The tribe as a political unit, so common elsewhere in America, did not exist in California. What we call a tribe was actually a number of groups of Indians, each of whom had a chief, spoke the same language dialect, had the same customs, intermarried regularly, and were usually mutually friendly. There was no tribal chief as such.

In the northwest portion of California wealth was so important that real chieftain leadership was lacking. In central and southern California the chief was a powerful local leader on a hereditary basis. Between the two extremes was a zone where tribes struck a compromise; the hereditary local chief had moderate authority and usually was well to do, but not necessarily so. Rich men in smaller political divisions were influential headmen under the local chief.

Warfare was only for revenge and not for plunder or for a desire for distinction. Except for the Northwest Sub-culture, scalps were generally taken and included the victim's skin down to his eyes or nose, and including the ears. Not infrequently the whole head was taken by a victorious warrior. The weapon was the bow and arrow, with rocks employed in close combat. Such war implements as shields, clubs, spears (throwing), and tomahawks were not used.

Guessing games, usually played by men, were universal, with variations, and heavy gambling was the rule. Shinny in several different forms was widely played.

Shamans were employed for curing diseases which were believed due to the presence in the body of some foreign hostile object. This was removed by sucking accompanied by singing, dancing, and tobacco smoking.

The girls' adulthood or puberty ceremony and dance was important to all California tribes.

Population figures even on the most scholarly basis, Kroeber states, are at best reasonable guesses. As nearly as can be determined there were originally about one million Indians in North America, three million in Central America, and three million in South America. California probably had about 133,000 Indians or nearly one per square mile. This is a density three or four times greater than for the whole of North America.

Today the North American Indian population (including about 30% half-breeds) is less than 10% of what it was. Over 90% of our Indians have been destroyed by wholesale killing at the hands of the white man, by new diseases, unfavorable changes in diet, clothing, and dwellings plus such Caucasian cultural factors as settlement, concentration, and the like. The decline in Indian population varied directly with the degree of civilized contact the several tribes experienced. It is interesting to note that virtually all of the Indians exposed to the Spanish missions commencing 1769 are gone except for a few in the extreme south who were only partly missionized. Kroeber states:

"It must have caused many of the fathers a severe pang to realize, as they could not but do daily, that they were saving souls only at the inevitable cost of lives. And yet such was the overwhelming fact. The brute upshot of missionization, in spite of its kindly flavor and humanitarian root, was only one thing: death."

Kroeber also points out that some tribes had much less resistance and hence suffered greater decline in population in response to equal white contact than others did. As in the case of other living things, there were favorable circumstances under which the Indian flourished---where life was relatively easy and secure. Such conditions produced virile stock and a rich culture both materially and spiritually---a condition found in broad valleys drained by the great rivers of California: the Klamath, the Sacramento, and the San Joaquin. As is also the case with specific plants and animals, Indians in less favorable sites lived submarginally---a difficult existence, poor in material and spiritual culture. Under such circumstances it takes just a small amount of additional unfavorable influence to make existence impossible. On this basis Kroeber explains the extinction or near extinction of poor mountain tribes upon contact with the whites while the Indians of the fertile valleys, although suffering more intensive Caucasian contact, were able to survive in reasonable numbers. This is a specific exception to the general observation made above that population decrease varied directly with the degree of contact. There are examples in California; the local one is the survival of valley Maidu and Wintun populations as compared to the surrounding mountain people with poorer cultures: the Yahi, Yana, Okwanuchu, Shasta, New River Shasta, Chimariko, and the Athabascan tribes of the west with survival percentages today of up to only 5% at best.

There is another factor which caused greater devastation of the economically insecure mountain tribes. White settlers were able to use to their own advantage some of the labor, services, and even food which the valley Indians afforded them. Thus it was not to the interest of the whites to wipe out these Indians. On the other hand, the mountain tribes with a poorer economy were prone to steal livestock to supplement their food supplies as they had no means to gain wealth to enable them to buy from the whites. Such depredations were a major cause of retaliation by white man in the form of bloody punitive attacks on Indians from whom the settlers had nothing to gain.

Chapter IV
INDIAN TRIBES OF THE LASSEN AREA

Lassen Peak with an elevation of 10,453 feet above sea level is the central high point of a somewhat topographically isolated mountain mass of volcanic origin. The slopes descending in all directions from Lassen Peak are clothed in coniferous forests, dotted with small lakes of glacial origin, and drained by a few fish bearing streams flowing radially from the mountain. There are also a few hot spring areas and some barren expanses where recent eruptions have produced mudflows and lavas. For the most part, game abounds in the Lassen highland, but the winters are snowy and severe, making it unsuitable for Indians to live there the year around.

As shown on the map, parts of the lands of four distinct tribes of Indians lay within what are today the boundaries of Lassen Volcanic National Park. Permanent homes and villages of Atsugewi, Yana, Yahi and mountain Maidu tribes were at lower elevations in the Ponderosa Pine and Digger Pine belts, and situated near streams. There food was relatively easily available and winters were the least severe within the limits of the respective tribal territories.

Each summer when deer migrated to higher elevations, the Indians also moved toward Lassen Peak to hunt and to fish trout, spending the whole summer in temporary camps.

There was some contact between the four tribes during their sojourns in the uplands of the park area, but the activities of each Indian group were pretty well confined to its own territory. The four Lassen tribes did on occasion engage in small battles, but this was the exception rather than the rule --- generally speaking they lived harmoniously as neighbors, and there was even occasional inter-marriage between tribes.

These tribes all had simple hill or mountain cultures which, in spite of some difrerence of custom, were surprisingly alike. It is believed that this is due to the fact that the four tribes all lived under very similar conditions of environment --- the same type of country in many respects. The similarity of their cultures is all the more interesting in that the Atsugewi were of the Hokan Family, speaking a Shastan language. Yana and Yahi, also of Hokan stock spoke Yana languages. The mountain Maidu were of the Penutian Family, speaking a Maidu language.

According to the best available figures, some of which are only

INDIAN TRIBAL AREAS OF THE LASSEN REGION
after A. L. Kroeber and T. R. Garth — — note the boundaries of
Lassen Volcanic National Park dashed in above and left of center
of the map. Lassen Peak is at the junction of the Atsugewi, Yana,
and Maidu territories.

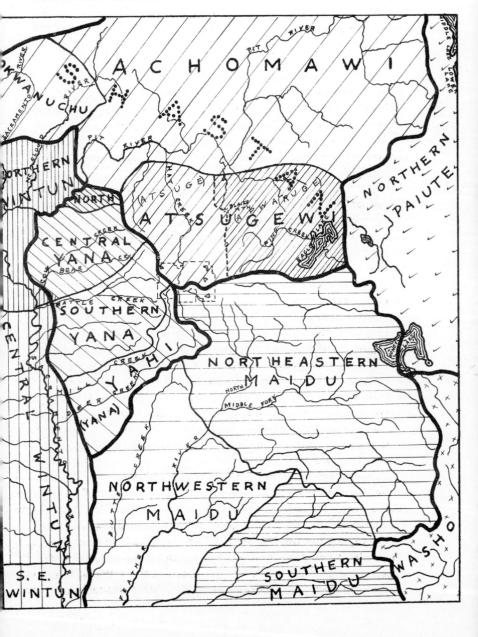

reasonable guesses, populations of the local tribes were probably about as follows:

	1770	1910	1950
Atsugewi	1,000	250	75
Yana (north, central, s)	750	25	10
Yahi	275	5	none
Maidu (mountain)	2,000	800	300
Totals	4,025	1,080	385

Garth states that: "The Atsugewi are divided into two major groups, the Atsuge or pinetree-people, who occupy Hat Creek Valley, and the Apwaruge--from Apwariwa, the name of Dixie Valley--who live to the east in and around Dixie Valley. Sometimes the Apwaruge are called Mahoupani, juniper-tree-people, a name which reflects the dry and barren nature of their territory . . . . . .

". . . . . . certain cultural differences (existed) between the eastern and western Atsugewi, who in most aspects of nonmaterial culture and in language are one people. In the western area there was more abundant rainfall and a fairly luxuriant growth of pines, oaks, and other trees. Here the Atsuge subsisted largely on acorns and fish; made twined basketry, using willow, pine root, *Xerophylum* grass, and redbud materials; and had bark houses and numerous other structures of bark. On the contrary, in the eastern area, which is comparatively arid and lacking in trees, the Apwaruge depended on the acorn less than did the Atsuge and fishing was less important, to judge by the scarcity or lack of nets, fish hooks, and harpoons; made inferior twined baskets of twisted tule with a different twist to the weave; as a rule had their houses covered with tule mats rather than with bark; and were much poorer than the Atsuge. This cultural distinction between the eastern and western areas is also found to the north among the Achomawi."

Dixon's studies have revealed that the Maidu had no general name for themselves, remarkable as this may seem. The name Maidu was first used by Stephen Powers in 1877 in his volume "TRIBES OF CALIFORNIA", a name he arbitrarily applied to these Indians since the word meant "Indian" or "man" in their language. The adjectives northwest or valley, northeast or mountain, and southern or foothill are applied to identify the three different cultures corresponding to the three distinct geographic provinces inhabited by the Maidu Indians as a whole. In a number of respects the culture of the mountain or northeast Maidu was more like that of their northern neighbors, the Atsugewi, than it was like that of the closely related southern and northwestern Maidu peoples. Obviously the factor of environment or characteristics of the land occupied is of extreme importance in creating such a situation.

Chapter V
INDIAN---PIONEER CONFLICT AND THE STORY OF ISHI

Conflict---prolonged, tragic, and violent---flared during the period when Europeans wrested control of North America from the native Indian. In viewing the struggle between Indian and white man, feelings run high even today.

What was it when Custer's contingent was wiped out? — when the Modocs inflicted such heavy losses on the American troops? — when the Navajo, Sioux, and others made their devastating raids on wagon trains and pioneer settlers? These were just as much a part of the war as were the exploits of Rogers' Rangers, the indiscriminate slaying of Indian men, women, and children in the Yahi caves on Mill Creek, and the annihilation of large segments of Atsugewi and Yana tribes cornered at points northwest of the present Lassen Volcanic National Park area. War is never a pretty thing. Was the hit and run killing of white people by Indians any less defensible morally than white man's atrocities against the Indians, or, for that matter, than commando raids and atomic bombings of today? Our viewpoint on such matters in the past has all too often been that might makes right, since we have always been on the winning side. Until very recently we have followed the biased opinion of the colonists and pioneers of these United States: whenever we won, it was a glorious and righteous victory, but if the Indian emerged victorious, it was regarded as a dastardly massacre. It is a viewpoint readily understandable where a person's loved ones are involved---but not justifiable.

Our veterans of recent wars will vouch for the fact that white man's wars can be primitive and violent when life and limb are at stake. We are hardly in a position to criticize the "cruel and sneaking" fighting methods of the Indians. Was it not use of Indian fighting methods which was so valuable to us in defeating the British in the colonial war for independence?

Indians fought in the only way they knew---and a disheartening losing fight it was for them with bows and arrows against rifles. For each gain in weapons and technical know-how the Indians made, the whites made many. True, it cost Americans much in the way of lives, anguish, and money, but how small were these losses in comparison to those of the Indians. American Indians, the undisputed owners of this continent for thousands of years, were not only nearly exterminated, but in the end we took virtually all of their land by force and with it took away the means of self support as well without "due process of law". We denied the Indian the right of "life, liberty, and the pursuit of happiness" --- the very things for which we as a nation stand. In all fairness, however, it should be stated that in recent years modest monetary retribution has been made by the U.S. Government to some of the surviving descendants.

S. F. Cook has pointed out that Spanish contact with California Indians was a rather passive matter. Spanish penetrated deeply, but did not settle on Indian lands of appreciable size. The Spanish were present in small numbers, a population numbering perhaps 4,000 by 1848. To be sure there was occasional bloodshed, but it was the exception in Spanish California rather than the rule, for the Spanish regarded Indians as an asset, a human resource which provided labor and even some food and materials. The Indians were a respected element in the social and economic structure of Hispanic California, having civic and legal rights. Even under the Spanish, was there a great reduction of the Indian population through limited warfare and displacement, but much more importantly through disease. Nevertheless, by 1845 a more or less satisfactory equilibrium seems to have evolved between the Spanish and the California Indians.

In contrast the hordes of white immigrants who followed considered the Indians entirely useless and there was no place for the latter in the pioneers' economy of material wealth. All good lands were taken from the Indians arbitrarily and as quickly as possible. However, it must be stated that there were exceptions to both the Spanish and Gringo relations with the California Indians, but, in general, the foregoing statements are accurate.

How the conflict of pioneer versus Indian affected the Atsugewi is summarized for us by Garth as follows:

"The Atsugewi, because of their somewhat secluded mountain habitat, were spared contact with white civilization until the middle of the nineteenth century. Although there were vague reports of contact with Spanish explorers or Mexican bandits, these could not be verified. Peter Skene Ogden may have been the first white man to visit the area (1827-1828). Besides the trappers, Fremont, Greenwood, and other explorers probably skirted Atsugewi country. Peter Lassen passed through Achomawi-Atsugewi country in opening the Pit River Route of 1848. He was soon followed by a stream of white migration from the east which was devastating to the Indians and their culture. Prospectors entered the Lassen region in

1851, and not long afterward came white settlers. By about 1859 the Indians were felt to be a menace to the whites in the area and were rounded up by militia and taken to the Round Valley Indian Reservation. Unsatisfactory conditions at the Reservation caused most of them to leave in 1863 and return to their old haunts along Hat Creek and Dixie Valley.

"Joaquin Miller reports an uprising in 1867 of the Pit River and Modoc Indians, who had made up old differences and were now fighting together. A number of whites were massacred. Miller speaks of an Indian camp being made on Hat Creek in the war that followed. It is not thus improbable that the Atsuge participated in that war. After a year or so of fighting the Indians suffered a final crushing defeat and surrendered. This last engagement may be the one at Six Mile Hill, spoken of by informants, in which a large number of their people were cornered in a cave and massacred by soldiers. After this, many of the Indians were again removed to Round Valley. Those remaining and some who subsequently returned from the Reservation maintained friendly relations with the whites. Today most Atsugewi live on allotments in their old territory, the younger Indians often working for their white neighbors or for the lumber mills. The census of 1910 gives a population of 240 for 'Hat Creek Indians'. This figure may also have included the Dixie Valley Atsugewi, since they are not mentioned in the census. The present population is probably half that or less."

The Maidu also were decimated upon contact with white man. However, with only rare exception, Maidu accepted rather passively invasion of their territory with the attendant driving away of game and destruction of fish in the streams by mining operations in gold rush days. However, since the remnants of the Maidu were in the way of white mans' developments, treaties were made in 1851 by which these Indians gave up all claims to their ancestral lands and were taken to short lived reservations in Amador, Nevada and Butte Counties, also later to the Round Valley Reservations in the Coast Range. A great many Maidu soon returned to their homes. In the late 50's and 60's a desultory war was waged on the Maidu by California State troops which further reduced the number of surviving Indians of this tribe.

The management of the University of California's excellent informative "UNIVERSITY EXPLORER" radio program series has given permission to quote the following from its broadcasts. This material concerns the conflict of the closely related Yana and Yahi tribes with the whites and the fabulous story of Ishi. The script has been abridged and considerably rearranged:

".... The Yana way of life was a strange one to the white observer, but the tribes prospered under it until white emigration from the East threw them into conflict with a new and unfriendly people. The Indians, of course, resented the white incursion and revolted against it. That happened in all sections of the country where whites displaced Indians, but it would be hard to imagine a more inept way of handling the situation than that used by the white men in the Sacramento Valley. Some of the large land owners protected the Indians of their holdings; among them were General John Bidwell, one of the founders of Chico, (Peter Lassen on his Rancho Bosquejo between Mill and Deer Creeks), and John Sutter, on whose property the Gold Rush started. But they were exceptions. Most of the settlers apparently believed the only way to handle the natives was to compete with them in cruelty. One celebrated Indian-killer took great pride in a blanket he had made from Indian scalps. The whites had learned scalping from the Eastern Indians, but they themselves popularized it in California. . . . .

"The Indians often plundered settlers' cabins and stole livestock. This was natural, since they regarded the whites as invaders. Unfortunately, the settlers' retaliation frequently consisted of rounding up a gang of Indians and slaughtering them. And it didn't make too much difference whether they were the guilty Indians. Professor Waterman wrote that the Yahi expressed their resentment of the white men more violently than did the other Yana groups, but since the Yahi moved around more and displayed greater skill in hiding out, quite innocent groups of Indians often took the blame for the acts of the Yahi. Professor Waterman cited the case of one white posse which took to the trail following a series of Indian raids. The posse came upon an encampment of Indians and shot about forty of them. But the Indians had been camped in the same place for two nights, and the whites later found a couple of almost-empty whiskey barrels there. It doesn't stand to reason, Professor Waterman pointed out, that Indians skilled in warfare would be so careless after an attack on their enemies.

"As the animosity between white men and red men grew, the atrocities on both sides became revolting. White women and children were tortured and killed by the Yana. But the anthropologists who have studied this unpleasant phase of California history believe the whites invited such savage assults by their own brutal mistreatment of the Indians.

". . . . The Yana gradually took to the woods as it became obvious that they were being outnumbered and decimated by the settlers in one massacre after another. By the late 1860's the Indians had been reduced in numbers and intimidated to the point where they no longer could be considered a serious menace to the people who had taken over their hunting grounds. By then the Indians' crimes were more on the level of petty theft than major violence. The three Yana tribes had become almost extinct as social organizations, but a fair number of Yana-speaking individuals survived long after the turn of the century.

"With the Yahi tribe, however, it was a different story. For a long time the Yahi---then called the Mill Creeks, because area around that little stream was their principal hunting ground---for a long time, the Yahi were believed to have been wiped out in a final massacre in 1865. . . . In 1871, a group of cattle-herders in Tehama County found a spot where Indians apparently had wounded a steer. The whites used dogs to follow the steer's bloody trail, and cornered some thirty Indians in a hillside cave. They promptly slaughtered the Indians, including several children. The settlers' peculiar idea of mercy was pointed out by Professor Waterman's informant, who noted that one of the cattle-herders could not bear to kill the children with his .56 caliber rifle--- 'it tore them up so bad' he said. So he did it instead with a .38 caliber revolver. . . . They call the rock shelter Kingsley Cave after Norman Kingsley, the settler who . . . . supposedly . . . . shot the Indian children. The Kingsley Cave site was apparently used for a long time. Grinding tools of two different cultural periods were found . . . . (by University of California Archeological Survey staff excavations currently investigating the site).

(The Yahi were thought to have been completely wiped out by this last unjustified atrocity, but in 1908) ". . . . surveyors for a power company in the hilly country around Deer Creek reported they had caught a glimpse of a naked Indian standing poised near the stream with a double-pronged primitive fishing spear. Next day, other members of the party were startled when an arrow came whistling through the underbrush at them

--- a stone-tipped arrow like those used by the supposedly extinct Indians. The surveyors kept on pushing ahead, until they came upon a cleverly concealed camp in the tangled woods. There they found a middle-aged woman and two aged and feeble Indians, a man and a woman. The old woman, hiding under a pile of rabbit skins, apparently wanted water, and the surveyors gave her some after the old man and the other woman had hidden in the underbrush. The surveyors also carried off all the blankets, bows and arrows and other articles in sight; but when they returned next day to make some sort of restitution, the Indians had disappeared. They were never seen again, even though the University later sent anthropologists in search of them. . . .

". . . . with the dawn of a clear August day in 1911. . . . The butchering crew of a slaughterhouse near Oroville were awakened . . . . by a furious barking of the dogs at the corral. They rushed into the corral to find a man crouching in the mud, surrounded by the slaughterhouse shepherd dogs. The butchers called off the dogs to get a closer look at their guest --- and a most unusual guest he was.

"The man's only clothing was a piece of torn, dirty canvas across his shoulders. His skin was sunburned to a copper brown, his hair was clipped close to the skull, and he obviously was suffering from severe malnutrition. His body was emaciated and his cheeks clung to the bones to accentuate his furiously glaring eyes.

"But the strangest thing about this man was his speech. It was like nothing the butchers had ever heard. . . . The sheriff tried English and Spanish, then several Indian dialects. But he was unable to draw any intelligible response from his prisoner. For lack of a better place to put him, the sheriff locked him in the jail cell reserved for mental cases, even though the man from the slaughterhouse appeared to be more lost than insane.

"The 'Wild Man of Oroville' made good newspaper copy, and clippings about his mysterious discovery caused much excitement in the department of anthropology at the University of California. It was a good thing that the news reached the University when it did. The frightened wild man was cowering in his cell, refusing to accept food from his captors whom he obviously distrusted, while the sheriff vainly tried to identify him.

"The late Professor T. T. Waterman was especially ex-

cited. So excited, in fact, that he stuffed a few clothes in
his suitcase, quickly picked out a list of words from the files
on California Indian languages, and caught the first train to
Oroville for an interview with the prisoner.

"The reason for Professor Waterman's excitement was that
he believed the Oroville prisoner was a Yahi Indian. If this
guess was correct, Waterman would have a major anthropological find. For anthropologists are concerned with origins,
development and variegated cultures of mankind; and if the
frightened prisoner in Oroville turned out to be a Yahi, Professor Waterman and his colleagues would have a living
encyclopedia of the language, customs, and habits of a people
who were believed to be extinct . . . . he might be one of the
little band reported at Deer Creek (in 1908), perhaps the man
with the fishing spear.

"The task of determining whether the prisoner was Yahi was
complicated by the fact that no one knew the Yahi language.
This doesn't sound like an insuperable stumbling block, until
you remember that the California Indian languages were
numerous and distinct; there were over one hundred dialects,
many of them mutually unintelligible. These dialects were
classified into eighteen major language groups, which in turn
made up six entirely different language families. These six
language families apparently are completely unrelated---a
strange circumstance, when you consider that almost all of
the languages of Europe can be traced to common origins.

"However, Professor Waterman was fortunate in one respect. A fairly extensive word-list had been collected from
the dialect of the Nozi Indians who had once lived just to the
north of the Yahi and were their nearest relatives. Both the
Yahi and the Nozi belonged to the Yana language stock, which
stemmed from the widespread Hokan family. So Professor
Waterman relied on Nozi words to make the identification.

"At first, the prisoner in Oroville seemed as frightened
of Professor Waterman as he had been of all the other white
men. Patiently, the anthropologist proceeded through his list
of Nozi words, but the captive Indian apparently recognized
none of them. At last, though, the professor pointed to the
wooden frame of the Indian's cot, and pronounced the word
'si'wi'ni,' which according to his list meant 'yellow pine'.
Immediately, the Indian relaxed. His harried, unhappy look
turned to beaming good cheer, and he acted as if he had found
a long-lost friend. Pointing to his cot, he repeated Pro-

fessor Waterman's word 'si'wi'ni' several times, as if agreeing that, yes, his cot was yellow pine. His own language differed from that of the Nozi, but some of the vocabulary was the same. Professor Waterman had struck upon one of the right words; later, he pronounced more familiar words, and it was established that the Indian was a Yahi. He also managed to explain that he called himself 'Ishi', which meant simply, 'I am a man'.

"Professor Waterman was naturally elated with his new-found acquaintance. The Butte County sheriff was equally elated to be rid of his difficult charge, so Ishi was taken to the Museum, then located in San Francisco, for further study and interrogation.

"Thus it happened that this human relic of the Stone Age came to live at a modern university. The Regents of the University gave Ishi some official status by appointing him an assistant janitor at $25 a month. But his value to the University did not come from dexterity with a mop and broom; he was valued because he could tell the anthropologists about his people, preserving knowledge which otherwise would have died with his fellow-tribesmen.

"Ishi adapted himself well to this new life, and he was a friendly and popular fixture at the museum for five years. He picked up the white man's ways by watching the people around him; at his first civilized dinner, he imitated his hosts' motions and managed a knife and fork far more skilfully than most of us can handle chopsticks in a Chinese restaurant. He was delighted and awe-stricken by many of the developments of civilization; but the things that impressed him most were not what the anthropologists had expected. Electric lights, airplanes, and automobiles made little impression; they were completely beyond his range of experience, and he dismissed them as 'white man's magic', worthy of little attention. The tall buildings in downtown San Francisco did not startle him; as he explained, his own country had cliffs and crags just as high. But what really amazed him about the city. were the enormous crowds of people on the streets. He had seen people before, of course, but never more than twenty or thirty in one place.

"In general, the things that Ishi considered most remarkable were things which approached something in his own experience. He knew how hard it was to start a fire by friction, so pocket matches were indeed a wonder. Water faucets

which could be turned on and off were likewise marvelous;
why, the white man could make a spring, right there in the
house! One of the first modern devices to catch Ishi's babbled
attention was an ordinary window roller shade. He tried to
push it aside, but it flipped back; he lifted it, but it fell down.
Finally someone showed him how to give it a little tug and
let it roll itself up, and Ishi was amazed. A half-hour later,
he was still trying to figure out what had happened to the
shade.

"Ishi and his hosts learned to communicate with each other
fairly adequately; he never became accustomed to formal
grammar, but he picked up a vocabulary large enough to ex-
press his wishes and his comments about the things around
him. Actually, the anthropologists admitted, Ishi learned to
speak English far better than any of them were able to learn
Yahi. They suspected that some of his vocabulary was
acquired from the school children who used to visit him, for
it included a fair sampling of most unacademic slang.

"There were some things Ishi didn't like to talk about
---the death of his relatives and the last horrible years around
Deer Creek before he wandered to the Oroville slaughterhouse
---were subjects he found too painful. Besides, there was
a tribal taboo against mentioning the names of the dead. His
close-cropped head, incidentally, was the result of burning
off his hair in mourning for his mother and sister, in accord-
ance with tribal custom.

"But the knowledge which Ishi passed on was rich and
varied. . . . Among the contributions for which Ishi is remembered are some of the finest arrowheads and spear tips in
existence; he made these for the University Museum both of
modern bottle glass and from the natural materials. . . . In
fact, Ishi was the source of almost all that is known of Yahi
life. He gladly described the customs of his people, and he
enjoyed chipping out Stone Age weapons and showing how
they were used. With primitive drawings, he tried to tell the
story of the massacre which wiped out most of his tribe. . . .

"Ishi's own life ended in March 1916, when he died of
tuberculosis. He was then believed to be in his 50's. Those
who knew him at the University considered his death a great
loss---not only because of what he had contributed to
anthropology, but because he had a natural friendliness and
dignity which made him a beloved personality. Professor
A. L. Kroeber once told me: 'The manner in which he acquitted

himself, both from the scientific and social points of view, was so admirable that everyone who chanced to meet him counted it a privilege to be his friend'. And Ishi had the comforting knowledge that his departure from this earth would not be a completely alien one. Because he had passed on the elements of his culture, it was possible to bury him with all the ceremony of his own people. His bows and arrows were laid beside him, and some bowls of food were placed in the grave so he would not grow hungry on his long journey to the Happy Hunting Ground. . . .

"Ishi was not only the last survivor of the Yahi . . . . but he was also believed to (have been) the last representative of the Stone Age in the United States."

While not apropos to the subject of this chapter, "Pioneer Conflict . . . ." we digress with some quotations from Pope's "Medical History of Ishi" to give the reader a better understanding of this last of the Mill Creek Indians, his character, and his beliefs.

". . . . Ishi himself later made the statement that he was not sick but had no food. White men had taken his bow and arrows; game was scarce, and he had no means of procuring it. He had strayed from his usual trail, between Deer Creek and . . . . Lassen (Peak). The railroad on one side and a large river on the other kept him from making his way to the refuge of the hills. His fear of trains and automobiles seems to have been considerable in those days.

"Upon being captured, Ishi, according to his own account, was handcuffed, confronted by guns and pistols, and intimidated to such an extent that he vomited with fear. . . .

"About this time (fall, 1912) I became instructor in surgery in the University Medical School, and thus came in contact with the Indian.

"From the first weeks of our intimacy a strong friendship grew up between us, and I was from that time on his physician, his confidant, and his companion in archery. . . .

"The Museum (of Anthropology) is near the Hospital, and since Ishi had been made a more or less privileged character in the hospital wards, he often came into the surgical department. Here he quietly helped the nurses clean instruments, or amused the internes and nurses by singing his Indian songs, or carried on primitive conversation by means of a very complex mixture of gesture, Yana dialect, and the few scraps of English he had acquired in his contact with us.

"His affability and pleasant disposition made him a uni-

versal favorite. He visited the sick in the wards with a gentle
and sympathetic look which spoke more clearly than words.
He came to the women's wards quite regularly, and with his
hands folded before him, he would go from bed to bed like a
visiting physician, looking at each patient with quiet concern
or with a fleeting smile that was very kindly received and
understood.

"ISHI'S MEDICAL BELIEFS"

"Women---Ishi had many of our own obsolete superstitions
regarding women. One critcism he made of white man's civilization was the unbridled liberty we give menstruating
women. The 'Sako mahale', as he designated them, were a
cause of much ill luck and s i c k n e s s. They should be in
seclusion during this period. In fact, he often commented on
the number of sick men that came to the hospital. I asked
him what he thought made so many men sick. He said it was
'Sako mahale, too much wowi (houses), too much automobile,'
and last but most important of all, the 'Coyote doctor', or
evil spirit.

"Dogs---Playing with dogs, and letting them lick one's
hand, Ishi said was very bad. He assured me that to let babies
play with dogs this way led to paralysis. It is interesting to
note that Dr. R. H. Gibson of Fort Gibson, Alaska, has reported the coincidence of poliomyelitis among the Tanana
Indians and the occurrence of distempers in dogs.

"Rattlesnakes---Ishi's treatment for rattlesnake bite was
to bind a toad or frog on the affected area. This is interesting
in the light of the experiments of Madame Phisalix of the
Pasteur Institute, who demonstrated the antidotal properties
of salamandrin, an extract obtained from salamander skin,
and the natural immunity that the salamander has to viper
vemon. Macht and Able have obtained a similar powerful
alkaloid from the toad *Bufo nigra,* called bufogin, which has
some of the properties of strychnin and adrenalin. It has been
used as an arrow poison by South American aborigines. Experiments which I conducted with salamandrin as an antidote
to crotalin, show that it has a pronounced protective and
curative value in the immunization of guinea pigs and in their
cure after being bitten by the rattlesnake. It is, however, too
dangerous and potent a poison itself to be of any practical
value.

"When out camping we killed and cooked a rattlesnake or

'kemna'. Ishi refused not only to taste it, but also to eat from the dishes in which it had been cooked. We ate it, and found that it tasted like rabbit or fish. Ishi expected us to die. That we did not do so he could only explain on the grounds that I was a medicine man and used magic protection.

"Moon---Ishi held the superstition common among uneducated Caucasians, that it is unwholesome to sleep with the moon shining on one's face, so he covered his head completely under his blankets when sleeping in the open.

"Hygiene---Ishi had wholesome notions of hygiene. When out hunting he has several times stopped me from drinking water from a stream which he thought had been contaminated by dwelling houses above.

"His residence in the Museum caused many misgivings in his mind. The presence of all the bones of the dead, their belongings, and the mummies were ever a source of anxiety to him. He locked his bedroom door at night to keep out spirits. When we stored our camping provender temporarily in the Museum bone room, Ishi was not only disgusted but genuinely alarmed. It was only after the reassurance that the 'bunch a mi si tee' could not enter through the tin of the cans that he was relieved.

"Surgery---On some of his visits to the University Hospital, Ishi gazed through the glass-panelled door of the operating room and watched the less grewsone scenes therein, wondering no doubt what was the meaning of this work . . . . and his questions afterward, though few and imperfectly understood, showed that he marveled most at the anaesthetic and that he debated the advisability of such surgical work.

"Once he saw me remove a diseased kidney. He viewed the sleeping man with deep wonder. He seemed interested at the methods we employed to prevent hemorrhage. For days afterwards he asked me if the patient still lived, and seemed incredulous when I said he did. When he saw an operation for the removal of tonsils he asked me why it was done. I told him of the pain and soreness which was indicative of disease, and necessitated the operation. He conveyed to me the information that among his people tonsilitis was cured by rubbing honey on the neck, and blowing ashes down the throat through a hollow stick or quill; no operations were necessary.

"The only surgical operation with which he seemed familiar was scarification. This was accomplished by means of small flakes of obsidian and had as its purpose the strengthening of the arms and legs of men about to go out on a hunt.

"Herbs---His own knowledge of the use of medicinal herbs was considerable, as we learned later when he went back to Deer Creek canyon with us on a three weeks' camping trip, here he designated scores of plants that were of technical, medicinal, or economic value. But he put very little faith in these things. The use of herbs and drugs seems to have been the province of old women in the tribe.

"There was a hole in the septum of his nose which he had used as a receptacle for a small piece of wood, as well as for holding ornaments. When he had a cold he placed in this spot a twig of baywood or juniper, and indicated to me that this was medicine. It served very much with him as menthol inhalers do with us. Its influence was largely psychic but agreeable.

"Magic--- The real medicine was magic. The mysteries of the k'uwi, or medicine man, were of much greater value than mere dosing. Their favorite charms seem to have been either blowing of smoke and ashes in certain directions to wield a protective or curative influence, or the passing of coals of fire through themselves or their patients by means of slight of hand. They also sucked out small bits of obsidian or cactus thorns from their clients, averring that these were the etiological factors of sickness.

"The principal cause of pain, according to Ishi, was the entrance of these spines, thorns, bee stings, or, as he called them, 'pins', into the human frame. The medicine man sucked them out, or plucked them while they were floating in the air in the vicinity of the sick man. They were then deposited in a small container, usually made of the dried trachea of a bird, or of a large artery. The ends of this tube were sealed with pitch or some form of a stopper and the whole thing taken possession of by the doctor, thus keeping the 'materia morbosa' where it could do no further harm.

"The fact that I was able to do sleight of hand: vanish coins, change eggs into paper, swallow impossible objects at will, and perform similar parlor magic, convinced Ishi that I was a real doctor, much more than any medication or surgery at my command. He came, nevertheless, to our clinic whenever he had a headache, or a bruised member, or lumbago, and accepted our services with due faith.

"ISHI'S PERSONAL HABITS"

"Sleep--- . . . . he slept between blankets in preference to sheets. He had several flannelette nightshirts but he preferred to sleep naked. . . .

"Clothing--- . . . . At first he was offered moccasins, but refused to wear them. He wanted to be like other people. Usually he wore a bright colored necktie and sometimes a hat, when he was going down town . . . . cotton shirts and (cotton) trousers were his choice. He used a pocket handkerchief in the most approved manner, and because of his frequent colds he needed it often.

"Modesty---Ishi, strange to say, was very modest. Although he went practically naked in the wilds, and, as described by Waterman, upon his first appearance in Deer Creek Canyon he was seen altogether nude, nevertheless, his first request after being captured was for a pair of overalls. He was quite careful to cover his genitalia; when changing clothes, assumed protective attitudes, and when swimming in the mountain streams with us wore an improvised breech clout even though his white companions abandoned this last vestige of respectability.

"Toilet---When well he bathed nearly every day, and he always washed his hands before meals. He was very tidy and cleanly in all his personal habits. When camping, he was the only man in our outfit who got up regularly and bathed in the cold mountain stream every morning.

"Ishi was an expert swimmer. . . . He used a side stroke and sometimes a modified breast stroke, but no overhand or fancy strokes; nor did he dive. He swam under water with great facility and for long distances. The rapids of Deer Creek were rather full yet he swam them, and carried my young son hanging to his hair.

"When he was sick he resented being bathed except when ordered by the nurse or doctor. Like many other primitive people, he considered bathing injurious in the presence of fever. He never attempted to take a sweat bath while in civilization, but often spoke of them. I never saw him brush his teeth, but he rubbed them with his finger, and they always seemed clean. He washed his mouth out with water after meals.

"His beard was sparse but he plucked it systematically by catching individual hairs between the blade of a dull jackknife and his thumb. In his native state he used a sort of tweezers made of a split piece of wood. He did this work without the use of a mirror.

"He combed and brushed his hair daily. He washed it frequently. . . . At first he had no dandruff, but after two or three years' contact with the whites he had some dry seborrhoea, and began to get a trifle gray at the temples . . . . he used grease on his scalp when in his native state; whereas bay leaves and bay nuts he said were heated and reduced to a semi-solid state, when they were rubbed on the body after the sweat bath. Here they acted as a soporific, or, as he said, like whiskey, and the person thus anointed fell into a sweet slumber. The same substance was rubbed on moccasins to make them waterproof.

"On one occasion he contracted ring worm, probably from a wandering cat. He was given a sulphur salve for this, and after its cure he still used the ointment to soften his hands. . . He was not susceptible to 'poison oak' . . . . nor to sunburn. His skin bleached out considerably while in San Francisco, and became darker when exposed to sunlight.

". . . . (he) seemed to have the same fondness for sweet-scented soap that Orientals manifest.

"His personal belongings he kept in a most orderly manner, everything in his box being properly folded and arranged with care. Articles which he kept outside of this box he wrapped in newspaper and laid in systematic arrangement on shelves in his room.

"In working on arrows or flaking obsidian, he was careful to place newspapers on the floor to catch his chips. In fact, neatness and order seemed to be part of his self-education.

"In the preparation of food and the washing of dishes he was very orderly and clean.

"Diet --- . . . . After a certain period of this luxury (eating heavily) he discerned the folly of this course and began eating less, when his metabolism returned to a more normal balance. Part of this increase was due to the large quantities of water he drank. Being unaccustomed to salt, our seasoning was excessive and led to increased hydration of his bodily tissues. He had a great fondness for sweets. . . . He tried and liked nearly all kinds of foods, but seemed to have an aversion for custards, blanc manges, and similar slimy confections, nor could he be persuaded to drink milk. He contended that this was made for babies, while he said that butter ruined the singing voice. . . .

"Matches he took up with evident delight; they were such a contrast to the laborious methods of the fire drill, or of nursing embers, which he employed in the wilds.

". . . . His meat he boiled only about ten minutes, eating it practically without seasoning.

"His own food in the wilds seems to have been fish, game, acorn meal, berries, and many roots. Prominent among these latter was the bulb of the *Brodiaea*. The Indian could go out on an apparently barren hillside and with a sharp stick dig up enough *Brodiaea* bulbs in an hour to furnish food for a good meal. These roots are globular in shape, with the appearance of an onion, ranging in size from a cherry to a very small potato. The flavor when raw is like that of a potato, and when cooked like a roasted chestnut.

"Alcohol --- . . . . Ishi himself had no liking for strong drink, although at one time he purchased a few bottles of beer and drank small quantities diluted with sugar and water. He called it medicine. His response to my query regarding whiskey was, 'Whiskey-tee crazy-aunatee, die man.'

"Tobacco---Occasionally Ishi smoked a cigarette, and he knew the use of tobacco, having had access to the native herb in the wilds. But he seldom smoked more than a few cigarettes a day, and frequently went weeks without any. He disapproved of young people smoking. He chewed tobacco at times, and spat copiously. Both of these indulgences, however, he resorted to only when invited by some congenial friend.

"Etiquette--- Although uncultured, he very quickly learned the proper use of knife, fork, and spoon. His table manners were of the very best. He often ate at my home, where he was extremely diffident; watched what others did and then followed their examples, using great delicacy of manner. His attitude toward my wife or any other woman member of the household was one of quiet disinterest. Apparently his sense of propriety prompted him to ignore her. If spoken to, he would reply with courtesy and brevity, but otherwise he appeared not to see her.

"When he wanted to show his disapproval of anything very strongly, he went through the pantomine of vomiting.

"Thrift---As janitor in the Museum, he was making a competent income, understood the value of money, was very thrifty and saving, and looked forward to the day when he could buy a horse and wagon. This seemed to be the acme

of worldly possession to him. He was very happy and well
contented, working a little, playing enough, and surrounded
by friends.

"ISHI'S DISPOSITION AND MENTALITY"

"Disposition---In disposition the Yahi was always calm
and amiable. Never have I seen him vehement or angry. Upon
rare occasions he showed that he was displeased. If someone
who he thought had no privilege touched his belongings, he
remonstrated with some show of excitement. Although he had
lived in part by stealing from the cabins of men who had
usurped his country, he had the most exacting conscience
concerning the ownership of property. He would never think
of touching anything that belonged to another person, and
even remonstrated with me if I picked up a pencil that belonged to one of the Museum force. He was too generous with
his gifts of arms, arrow-heads, and similar objects of his
handicraft.

"His temperament was philosophical, analytical, reserved,
and cheerful. He probably looked upon us as extremely smart.
While we knew many things, we had no knowledge of nature,
no reserve; we were all busy-bodies. We were, in fact,
sophisticated children.

"His conception of immortality was that of his tribe, but
he seemed to grasp the Christian concept and asked me many
questions concerning the hereafter. He rather doubted that
the White God cared much about having Indians with Him, and
he did not seem to feel that women were properly eligible to
Heaven. He once saw a moving picture of the Passion Play.
It affected him deeply. But he misconstrued the crucifixion
and assumed that Christ was a 'bad man'.

"Use of tools---He was quite adept in the use of such
simple tools as a knife, handsaw, file, and hatchet. He early
discovered the advantages of a small bench vise, and it took
the place of his big toe in holding objects thereafter. . . .
Journeys were measured by days or sleeps . . . . (he) was
awe-struck when I took him to a sawmill where large cedar
logs were brought in and rapidly sawed up into small bits to
be used in making lead pencils. It would have taken hours
for him to fell even a small tree, and an interminable length
of time to split it. But here was a miracle of work done in a
few minutes. It impressed him greatly. . . ."

In concluding remarks on Indian conflict with pioneer, a word concerning Indian reservations will not be amiss. The author does best again in quoting, this time from Kroeber:

"The first reservations established by Federal officers in California were little else than bull pens. They were founded on the principle, not of attempting to do something for the native, but of getting him out of the white man's way as cheaply and hurriedly as possible. The reason that the high death rate that must have prevailed among these makeshift assemblages was not reported on more emphatically is that the Indians kept running away even faster than they could die.

"The few reservations that were made permanent have on the whole had a conserving influence on the population after they once settled into a semblance of reasonable order. They did little enough for the Indian directly; but they gave him a place which he could call his own, and where he could exist in security and in contact with his own kind. . . ."

Despite certain undesirable features of Indian Reservations, the general conclusion is that for a number of tribes survival has been considerably greater today than would have been the case if the Indians had had to shift for themselves in competition with the whites.

Chapter VI
HUNTING

Hunting was obviously a very important activity of the Lassen Indians, not only for survival, but as a means of acquiring the comfort and security which success brought. Also a good hunter was held in high esteem socially.

Deer were most sought and the hunter went to considerable effort to get "deer power" (a sort of guardian spirit) to possess him. This gave him skill and good luck. Generally only men hunted, sometimes individually, at other times in small or large groups.

Before going hunting tobacco was often smoked ceremonially with prayers and singing while the shaman (medicine man) supervised and the hunters' bodies were anointed with medicine. Weapons to be used were smoked over a fire, while the hunters talked to their bows and arrows about the coming hunt. Frequently Atsugewi Yana, and Yahi hunters also cut themselves until they bled. This was true especially if their marksmanship had not been good of late. Cuts were made in the forearm and charcoal was rubbed in. They often took sweat baths too before hunting, but the Maidu did not. The latter, however, offered shell beads to help increase deer power. Atsugewi hunters left offerings of paint, tobacco, and eagle-down at certain spots in the mountains for luck.

After a youth killed his first game, Maidu and Atsugewi switched him, a bow string being commonly used. Then the Atsugewi father talked to his son, blew smoke on him, and sent him out alone into the mountains for at least five days to seek power. Yana and Yahi youths were not permitted to touch, skin, or eat any of their first kill of each kind of animal, lest it spoil their luck. In these tribes the father skinned the animal and dressed the hide, teaching his son how this was done.

After hunting there were often cleansing activities and ceremonies, and usually a division of meat although a lone hunter could retain all of it. It was considered quite bad to come home empty handed. After a bear had been killed he was spoken to kindly and in sympathetic terms. Deer eyes were often eaten to give good sharp eyesight to the eater.

In a popular method of deer hunting by all Indians of the Lassen area, a deer head disguise was worn by the hunter. He approached his quarry cautiously using screening bushes and moving his antlered head above them to simulate a buck feeding. Sometimes the hunter carried brush along in front of himself. The mountain

Maidu always used the whole deerskin for disguise. When close enough the hunter would shoot with bow and arrow. Since this was a nearly silent weapon, there was no noise to startle the deer, and so it was sometimes possible to slay two or three deer on one occasion.

Atsugewi hunters might encircle a small brush covered or wooded mountain. They set many fires, leaving non-burning gaps where bowmen hid in holes. The deer were shot as they came out of the burning area.

Mountain Maidu sometimes concealed themselves in pits near deer licks where they shot the animals in moonlight.

Another hunting method was to drive deer along fences built of brush or stone or along ropes to which bunches of tules were tied as hanging streamers. Strategically placed hunters in shallow pits shot the driven deer as they passed through openings which had been left. Dogs were frequently used in hunting out and in driving deer.

The brush deer-blind along a well traveled deer trail was used too, as well as hanging a noose in the deer trail to snare the deer. Still another means of taking deer was like that of the northern neighbors of the Atsugewi, the Pit River Tribe or Achomawi. They employed a six or seven foot deep pit about nine feet long dug with slightly undercut side walls. This opening was covered and concealed with poles, brush, and dirt. As the deer trotted along established trails over the disguised pitfalls they fell through. Or, deer might be driven to such pits, sometimes with the aid of converging walls or fences in conjunction with pitfalls. Deer trapped in these pitfalls were killed by strangling from above with ropes.

Another popular way to secure deer was to follow the animal for one or more days. The pursuing Indian carried a small amount of food which he ate to sustain himself while moving. The deer, although swifter afoot than the hunter, was persistantly followed at a steady pace. The animal did not get a chance to feed properly nor to rest. At length the deer became weakened to the point where the hunter could approach and shoot it at close range.

If a hunter were fairly close to a deer and it was moving, he might shout at it, causing the deer to stop momentarily out of curiosity. This provided a better chance of bringing the quarry down with bow and arrow. Deer were sometimes lured closer by whistling with lips, blowing on a leaf or grass blade held in the hands, or by imitating the cry of a fawn. A hunter is said occasionally to have been able to sing to a group of deer, holding their attention while he cautiously approached within arrow range.

If practical, deer or other game was killed by driving the animals over cliffs. Elk, mountain sheep, antelope, and reportedly occasionally even bison were hunted by one or more of the means. Except for the case of mountain sheep, such animals were probably rare within the territories of the tribes being considered.

Meat of such large game was prepared for eating after skinning by roasting in the earth pit ovens to be described in succeeding chapters or by cutting up and boiling. Much venison and the like was also stored for winter use. In this case the meat was cut into strips and dried in the sun or on wooden frames over fires. This was not a smoking, but rather a drying process. Such jerked meat was stored in large, tightly woven baskets. Meat fresh or dried was almost invariably eaten with acorn mush.

Bear hunting was common among tribes of the Lassen area. The American Black Bear is not aggressive and by no means always black. He is of moderately large size and often is light or dark brown in color. Indians liked to hunt the Black Bear in winter, two hunters entering the hibernating den. One carried a torch and the other a bow and arrow. They rolled a large block of wood in front of them and shot the bear at point blank range, then quickly ran out. Wounded, frightened, and in a semi-stupor, the bear usually stumbled over the wooden block. If he did not die in the den, but came out, he was shot by other waiting hunters. Mountain Maidu instead of entering the den smoked the bear out with pitchy torches planted at the den entrance.

The California Grizzly was much larger, fiercer, and more aggressive. This grizzly is now extinct, but was common especially in the foothill and lower mountain slopes of California before the coming of the white man. Grizzlies were normally engaged only by a large group of hunters and after considerable ceremonial preparation. Hunters never entered the den. Two stout poles were crossed in front of the opening with one or two men holding each --- a dangerous job. The bear was spoken to nicely and urged to come out which he usually soon did. As the bear started to climb over the poles at the den entrance, the Indians pushed up forcing the bear's body against the roof so that he could most easily be shot. If this maneuver was not successful, a brave hunter enticed the bear to pursue him while the others shot arrows into the grizzly. Especially sharp and heavily poisoned arrow points were used on grizzly bear by the Atsugewi.

It was believed that a man who drank fresh bear blood would be very healthy thereafter, if he were strong enough. If he were weak, however, drinking the blood would kill him promptly.

Mountain lion were tracked, sometimes with dogs, sometimes in the snow, then treed and shot. Wildcats were generally killed in the same way. A hunter might coax a mountain lion to leap at him by simulating a deer feeding, using the deer head and skin disguise, but this was a dangerous practice.

Except in the eastern part of Atsugewi territory where the Apwaruge lived, rabbits were not plentiful. Yana, Yahi, and Maidu hunted them more, driving cottontail, snowshoe, and jack rabbits into long nets and clubbing them to death. In the winter rabbits were sometimes tracked and shot with bow and untipped arrows.

Other small mammals were shot, caught by dogs, and dug, smoked, or drowned out of burrows. A stick split at the end was thrust into a burrow and by twisting was entangled in the creature's fur sufficiently to drag him out. Ground squirrels could be outrun and killed by stepping on them. Skunks, badgers, rats, and more often porcupines were eaten---the latter being clubbed or stoned to death.

Small and medium sized animals were also caught under stone or log deadfalls which were propped up to drop on the victim while it was traveling along a runway, crossing a stream on a log, or when the animal pulled on a baited trigger. Similar placing was used for setting spring snares which took advantage of bent tree limbs for power. Long fences with nooses placed in gaps were used for rabbits, quail, and the like, and on occasion for creatures as large as deer. Some nooses were even operated by hand from a place of hiding.

Birds of all sorts were caught too, but live or imitation decoys were never employed as lures. Woodpeckers were removed from the nest by hand or else a noose was hung around the nest opening. Some birds were taken in basketry traps. Waterfowl were shot with bow and arrow and the young were run down. Eggs were also taken. Some ducks were speared at night from canoes or driven into nets by use of a canoe with fire at one end. Frequently nets or snares were suspended at intervals just above a stream where waterfowl commonly alighted. Ducks and geese were also driven into the traps in taking off from the water.

Grouse and small birds like robins and blackbirds were shot with blunt or untipped arrows, usually of one-piece construction.

It is interesting to note that in contrast to other local tribes, the

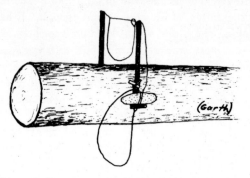

Atsugewi Snare set on a log lying across a stream.

Yana and Yahi tribes did not employ the following hunting techniques: burning brush, using bird snaring booths, nets for ducks, geese, rabbits, or deer, nor was game driven into enclosures or quail secured by use of net traps or drive fences. Futhermore Yana and Yahi did not believe that game was immortal.

It was not an uncommon practice, especially among the mountain Maidu, to frequently burn off their lands to make for easier travel and to minimize the possibility of ambush by enemies. The frequent "light" burnings do not seem to have generated enough heat to have destroyed the forests. Never the less this practice is not regarded as a wise conservation as it is definitely injurious to tree and much other plant reproduction as well as being destructive of organic material in the soil, damaging the watershed and being unfavorable to certain animal species, as well as accelerating erosion.

Chapter VII
FISHING

Fishes were one of the four important food categories consumed by Indians of the Lassen region. Land-locked and other non-migratory Rainbow Trout were abundantly available in mountain streams and in some lakes. Steelhead Trout penetrated the territories of our four tribes too. Salmon, however, did not go so far upstream, only rarely coming up Hat Creek, for instance, into Atsugewi lands. For the most part this tribe of Indians visited the Pit River to the north in the autumn. They paid the Achomawi, through whose territory this fine salmon stream flowed, for the privilege of catching salmon by giving up a share of the catch to them. The larger streams in south Yana, Yahi, and mountain Maidu country contained salmon and steelhead, but it seems that these tribes also made bargains with the Valley Indians for salmon fishing privileges or else made fishing forays to the Sacramento River.

Gill nets about three feet high and as much as 30 feet long were commonly used. Spawning trout in the spring were speared in large numbers. Although old informants have denied the practice, Boonookoo-ee-menorra (Mrs. Selina La Marr of the Atsugewi) tells of catching Rainbow Trout by hand from Manzanita Creek banks about fifty years ago when her family came up in the summer to fish. Trout were speared by the Atsugewi with two pointed or four

Atsugewi Bow-type net. This kind was usually used in small streams where it covered the full width of the stream bed. Fish were commonly driven into it, then the handle was raised.

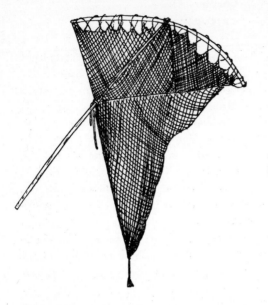

A northeast Maidu bow-fish net about forty inches long. It was used for fish other than salmon. Northwest and southern Maidu did not use such nets, employing seine nets instead (after Dixon)

pointed spears instead of the common single pointed version. Bone or Serviceberry wood might be used for the tips. Spears were used not only from stream banks, but, especially at night, from a canoe equipped with a torch in front. One man or more would spear the fish while a person, sometimes a woman, paddled the craft from the rear. The torch consisted of four mountain-mahogany sticks bound together with pitch down the center.

It is interesting to note that the practice of shooting fish with bow and arrow was not carried on by any tribes of the Lassen area, although the eastern people of the Pit River Indians (Achomawi), the western Shasta, Wintu, and foothill Maidu did do so.

Only Atsugewi, of the tribes we are considering, trapped fish in converging weirs into which fish might be driven. In the autumn, streams were sometimes diverted by damming. The fish trapped in the ponds remaining were scooped out with baskets or nets. Mountain Maidu drove fish into traps and caught lamprey eels in dip or scoop nets. Bow-type nets illustrated in the text were used with the bow bent ends down resting on the bed of the stream, the pole being raised to trap the fish. The net was preferably as wide as the stream.

All local tribes fished with lines and hooks which were made by lashing a sharp piece of bone to a section of twig, at an acute angle. Atsugewi and mountain Maidu also used a **"gorge"** for

A Klamath fish hook similar to those used by local tribes. Single barbed hooks were also employed.

angling. This was a slender piece of bone two or three inches long fastened near the middle and sharpened at both ends. Hooks were sometimes baited with meat, grasshoppers, or large flies, but man-made "flies" as fishermen know them today were not used. Sometimes meat or grasshopper bait was used by Atsugewi on fishlines without any hook. Atsugewi women occasionally fished with baskets and with hook and line. Hooks were often tied in a series on a line attached either on both banks of the stream or to a pole secured in the bank or tied to tules or to brush, and left over night. A series of basket traps was sometimes likewise stretched across a stream.

Salmon fishing was done largely with harpoons which differ from spears in having one or more movable barbs or toggles of bone. These opened when the harpoon was pulled back (outward in the victim) thus securing the catch all the more firmly. This was necessary for such large and heavy fish as salmon. Yana tribes caught their salmon with either hook and line or by spearing with a two pointed harpoon.

Natural falls were favored fishing sites. There Indians caught salmon and steelhead trout as the fish attempted to scale the falls. Long handled nets were used. Atsugewi went so far as to build scaffoldings to assist either in this method of fishing or from which to harpoon large fish. In the latter case many whitish rocks, where available, were thrown into the stream to build up a light colored bottom for better visibility in harpooning or spearing.

After the fish were caught they were killed by striking with a stick as a general practice. Mountain Maidu sometimes killed fish by striking their heads on rocks. The central Yana, interestingly enough, killed fish by biting them!

In quiet portions of streams fish were p o i s o n e d by placing certain pounded plant materials in the water. Yana and Yahi used crushed Soaproot; Atsugewi used pulverized Wild Parsley. Wild Parsley application made the water bluish, and caused the fish soon to rise to the surface of the water floating belly-up. Where suitable quiet pools did not exist in a stream, they were sometimes formed by the Indians through temporary damming. Buckeye nut pulp, which is poisonous, was not uѕed in this area for poisoning fish.

Long basketry fish traps, usually constructed by men, were also utilized. The design and proportions of these varied with the tribe.

Each of the Lassen area tribes had taboos which prevented youths, and in the case of Atsugewi, their parents too, from eating the first fish each youth caught.

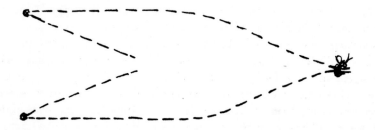

Plan of Maidu open basketry fish trap (after Dixon) several feet long. The pointed end was untied to extract the fish.

Chubs and minnows, spurned by white man, were driven into nets and eaten. At lower elevations, where waters were warmer and sluggish, suckers provided a common source of food fish. The Indians also not infrequently dove for crawfish and fresh water mussels. These were gathered in net sacks by male Indians of all local tribes. Yana and Yahi roasted mussels but did not boil them and never dried them for later use. A flat rock might be carried on the shoulders to assist the diving Indians.

Some fish were cooked by roasting over coals or by boiling. Most trout, however, were cleaned, head and backbone removed, and then strung up on poles to dry. No salt was used in the process. The dried fish was c a r r i e d to camp or v i l l a g e in large baskets. Dried trout was tied into small bales for storage and placed in baskets or in pits dug in the ground for safe-keeping. Salmon were usually cooked in earth pit ovens, then dried and

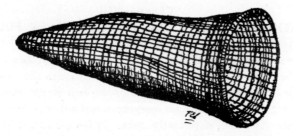

Atsugewi basketry fish trap (after Garth).

crumbed by Atsugewi and mountain Maidu for later use. This was of necessity an autumnal acitivity. Yana and Yahi stored their salmon in dried slabs, pulverizing it as needed.

Chapter VIII
GATHERING AND PREPARATION OF OTHER FOODS

As has been pointed out earlier under "California Indians", these tribes had a common food pattern. Although there was some difference in the relative importance of the four major types of food to the several tribes due to varying availability, the California Indians ate (1) game, especially deer, (2) fish, particularly salmon and trout, (3) roots and bulbs which the women dug, and (4) fruits and seeds of a wide variety, the most important of which were acorns.

Besides fish and venison, many kinds of flesh food were eaten by the Indians of the Lassen area: fox, wolf, grizzly and black bear, skunk, raccoon, porcupine, rabbit, owl, fish, fresh water mussel, and turtle being most common. They also ate with apparent relish a variety of insects and the like including crickets, grasshoppers, angleworms, red ant eggs, and yellow-jacket larvae.

Game which was not eaten by either Atsugei or mountain Maidu was coyote, elk, antelope, and all snakes and lizards. The last two items were almost universally shunned by California Indians. Many California tribes including Yana and Yahi refused to eat dog meat, some of them believing canine flesh to be poisonous. That mountain Maidu was one of the few tribes which ate dog flesh whenever it was available is denied by Dixon. Atsugewi ate it only as a last resort when rare, near-famine conditions prevailed or during times of severe epidemic. Canine flesh was believed by them to be a powerful and perhaps somewhat dangerous medicine. Buzzards seem to have been about the only birds which were not eaten.

Each tribe had certain taboos on eating game. An Atsugewi did not, for example, eat wildcat, gopher, hawk, lamprey eel, or caterpillars. Mountain Maidu did not eat mountain lion, badger, raven, or crawfish.

Heart of deer was taboo to all males among Atsugewi and to all children and youths of the mountain Maidu. The foetus of all animals and also deer fawns could not be eaten by any except Atsugewi, Yana, and Yahi old men and old women. Animal foetus was, however, allowed as food to all mountain Maidu adults. Bear foetus was skinned by Atsugewi and fed to old women because it was so tender. Likewise, Yana and Yahi made foetus soup for old folks to eat. Deer liver was taboo to Atsugewi boys and youths. Taboo also among Atsugewi was the eating of fish and deer meat together. Among mountain Maidu the eating of salt on bear meat was prohibited. Many other food combinations were outlawed by these and other California tribes.

Deer backbone was ground up and eaten dry by mountain Maidu or molded into small cakes, then baked and eaten while Atsugewi would dry deer backbones with meat still adhering, grind it up, and then boil the meal before eating it. Yana also ate pulverized meal of other bones after cooking. Marrow was relished; it was a special delicacy for Yana children.

Securing of large game and fish and their preparation has been described earlier.

Such animals as wildcat, raccoons, foxes, et cetera were skinned and cooked in earth ovens by all local tribes. These were pits sometimes as much as six feet wide and lined with rocks. A large fire was built in the pit to thoroughly heat the rock lining, after which any unburned debris was removed. The animal to be roasted was laid in the pit on a layer of green pine needles, or various other leaves, depending upon the tribe. A large heated rock was placed inside the body cavity and smaller hot rocks were wedged under the fore and hind legs which were then all tied tightly together. A flat heated rock might be placed on top of the carcass and the whole was covered with pine needles and the like, and finally with hot ashes and sometimes dirt. The roasting proceeded for half a day or so. Blood and fat might be placed in the intestine membranes of larger animals (especially wildcat) to form sausage and cooked in ashes. Mountain Maidu also boiled blood for eating.

Quills of porcupine and hair of badger, squirrel, or other small mammals might be singed off before cooking instead of skinning the animals. Ground squirrels were sometimes merely gutted and then roasted in ashes without further preparation. When Yana (and probably Yahi) did this, they then skinned the ground squirrels after cooking and mashed the whole bodies by pounding before eating them. Rabbits were roasted over coals and broken into pieces for eating. Both mountain Maidu and Atsugewi sometimes broiled small mammals on a single stick over coals.

Turtles were cooked alive in hot ashes. If they crawled out they were pushed back in again.

Duck eggs were boiled in baskets using hot rocks --- cooked they would keep for a week or two. Yana tribes roasted quail eggs in ashes. Birds were gutted, feathers singed off in flames and roasted on sticks or roasted in oven pits. Roasting was invariably used for the large birds such as ducks, geese, and swans.

Atsugewi practiced some fascinating gathering techniques in

in which they were not unique. Insects were gathered by both men and women. Grasshoppers and crickets not infrequently appeared in large numbers. These were collected early in the morning while still sluggish with cold. When very abundant they were scraped with sticks from branches of bushes into large burden baskets. During the heat of the day grasshoppers were effectively collected by singeing them. Some tribes merely burned dry grassy fields after which the insects were easily picked up. Atsugewi made a long willow "rope" to which many bunches of dry grass were fastened. This was set afire and men carrying this blazing band stretched tightly between them ran across open grassland where the grasshoppers were numerous. The insects jumped into the flames and were thus killed. Yana pulverized grasshoppers and other insects without cooking them.

Atsugewi roasted crickets in the pit oven. These were then dried two days and finally eaten or stored. If they had been stored, they were pounded before being eaten.

Salmon flies were plentiful along Pit River and Lost Creek (outside of the park). These were hand picked from the banks early in the morning. The wings were removed and the bodies boiled before eating by the Atsugewi.

When yellow-jackets, always carnivorous (meat eaters), were seen buzzing about, Atsugewi would tie a white flower petal to a grasshopper leg. When the yellow-jacket picked this morsel up and flew away with it toward its nest, the Indians would run after the yellow-jacket which was easy to follow on account of the conspiculus flower petal it carried along. Thus yellow-jacket nests were found. A line was marked around the nest area with the fingers. This line was supposed to increase the size of the nest. Pine needles were then stacked over the nest and burned to kill the winged insects. This done, the nest was dug up and roasted alongside a fire, thus cooking the maggot-like grubs inside. These were considered to be quite a delicacy. According to Dixon, mountain Maidu young folks were denied this delicacy, but not so among the Yana. Dried grasshoppers, crickets, and yellow-jacket larvae were foods often used as items of trade.

Angleworms were collected by first driving a digging stick a few inches into the moist soil, then moving the top about. The consequent disturbing of the ground made the worms crawl out. Although other California tribes made angleworm soup, Atsugewi, Yana, and probably Yahi sometimes roasted angleworms between hot rocks. Maidu reportedly dried worms for eating.

Red ant eggs were eaten by Indians too. Atsugewi baked them

A. Sharpened iron rod digging stick with pine cross piece wrapped in coarse cotton cloth used for about forty years by Mrs. Mullen of Hat Creek. Length about four feet.

B. Another recent mountain mahogany digging stick made by Mr. and Mrs. Lyman LaMarr (Boonookoo-ee-menorra) The point of the green wood was toughened in flame. Stick three and one half feet long.

in earth pit ovens, while mountain Maidu parched them with coals. Mountain Maidu also ate certain caterpillars, but the other tribes of the Lassen area did not.

Indians of this region did not carry on any agriculture, that is they did not plant crops for food or other purposes, but collected those which grew wild. It was, however, a common practice to burn some areas over regularly to stimulate growth of edible seed producing plants. Women always gathered the vegetable materials and prepared them for use.

Roots and bulbs provided vital foods to the aborigines also. These were procured with a digging stick. In this region it was blunt at the top with a tapered point at the digging end. Atsugewi fastened a short cross piece on top to serve as a handle. The digging stick was made by this tribe of green mountain-mahogany wood with the digging point hardened by scorching in the flame.

After the coming of white man, the same design was retained, but an iron rod replaced the mountain-mahogany digging shaft.

In use, the digging stick was thrust into the ground next to the plant whose root was to be secured. The handle portion was worked sideways a couple of times, then pulled downward toward the operator. The point very effectively brought the root out of the ground. Roots were customarily tossed into a large cone-shaped carrying basket which was held in place on the digging woman's back by a chest band over her chest. Some of the load in the basket might also be supported by a band from the basket over the Indian woman's forehead.

Roots were cleaned by rubbing (sometimes with sand) in a shallow bowl-shaped basket of a rough coarse mesh weave of willow ribs, like that used for cleaning acorns. The whole was dipped in water frequently. Rubbing usually continued until the skins were entirely removed.

The most important item of this type collected in large amount for food is known as epos locally, or "peh-ts-koo" among the old Atsugewi. The plant belongs to the parsley family and stands one to two feet high. Actually, probably more than one species was eaten by Indians of the Lassen area. These plants are not unlike except in detail. All had sweet carrot-like taproots about two inches long. Garth states that Atsugewi ate the species *Pteridendia bolanden* which apparently corresponds to the botanists' *Perideridia bolanderi* or *Eulophus bolanderi;* also probably *Carum* or *Perideridia oregona* and *californica.* Common English names for epos are squaw root or yampah. Epos roots were dried and stored, then ground up for use. This food item was made into either soup or bread. The finished product had a fine sweet meaty or nutty taste, and was held in high esteem. Obviously this constituted an important vegetable in the diet.

At least two kinds of *camas* bulbs and *brodeia* bulbs were roasted in the earth pit oven, ground to pulp, shaped into cakes, and rebaked. These were then either eaten or dried and stored. The latter process was not employed by mountain Maidu. If the baked camas cakes were stored, they would be soaked with water before eating. Camas cakes were not made into soup.

Tiger lily bulbs were roasted in earth pit ovens and eaten immediately. They were a highly prized food.

Wild onion was used too, but usually with other root foods as a flavoring.

The foregoing are but a few of the most extensively eaten roots.

Many others, especially those of the lily and parsley families, were used by tribes of the Lassen region.

Yana tribes robbed gophers of stores of edible roots and bulbs. These were found by probing for burrows and digging out the animals' food storage chambers. Men usually did this, which is an exception to the general rule that women only collected vegetable materials.

Acorns were probably the most important single food of California Indians. Surprisingly, this was true even in eastern parts of the territories of the Atsugewi (Apwaruge), mountain Maidu, and others where acorns were scarce or wanting entirely. Indians frequently traded for acorns or made long journeys for them. Acorns of the black oak were generally preferred over other kinds. Nearly all varieties were used for food on occasion, however. It is interesting to note that Modoc and Klamath Indians were exceptions in not using acorns for food.

In the fall, usually in September, acorns were gathered by women after the ripe nuts had been knocked from the oaks with long poles, or by men and young agile girls climbing the trees to strike the fruit with straight sticks or staves. To aid in climbing large smooth tree trunks, Atsugewi men used sapling ladders on which part of branches were left attached to serve for footholds. Mountain Maidu on the other hand used a very unique two poled ladder with buckskin rungs. Acorns were carried to villages by women in stages, using baskets about the size of nail kegs.

First spring food gathering each year was marked by rites in which the shamans, or medicine men, conducted praying ceremonies. Atsugewi conducted three of these. In May first epos roots were gathered and sung over by shamans. They examined the roots and prophesied whether the women who had dug them were going to be sick. Those who were going to be sick dug roots all day. In the evening these were dumped into piles and women shamans sang over these for half the night to make the threatened women healthy. Each woman gatherer participating then took home the roots she had dug leaving some for the shamans, who cooked and ate them. A second first food ceremony consisted of a ceremonial feast of fruit and vegetable materials with fish which the men brought. In the third such rite, root digging women threw away the first roots they dug that season and prayed to the effect: "Don't make me poor. Give me good luck. You may have this one."

In autumn, mountain Maidu held their first fruit ceremonies. Large groups of women went out to gather acorns. Acorn mush was made immediately of the first batch collected. The shamans ate

some and prayed. Portions of this batch were then eaten by the
rest of the assemblage. After that it was all right for anyone to
gather and to use acorns of the new crop.

Local tribes stored acorns in the shell either indoors in large
baskets or outside in pits or in large hoppers or granaries covered
with bark. The details of these varied with the several tribes.
Maidu except for the "mountain tribe" and Yana shelled, split,
and slightly dried some of their acorns, and placed them in basketry
storage bins lined with broadleafed maple leaves. Maidu ate
twelve different kinds of acorns, but the favorites were the black
oak *(Quercus kelloggii)*, *golden cup oak* maul, or canyon oak
(Quercus chrysolepis), and sierra live oak *(Quercus wislizenii)*
acorns.

In preparation, acorns were cracked by up-ending each on a
flat rock and striking the point with any convenient small stone.
Sometimes small acorns were cracked with the teeth. Though
usually a woman's job, young folks and men might help with the
task.

The thin brownish skin which covers the acorn kernels was removed by rubbing vigorously in rough porous baskets made entirely
of willow ribs. Water was not used. Indians of the Lassen area
did not employ stone mortars for grinding acorns as was the practice
in other parts of California. Stone mortars were always found, not
made, and were used for ceremonial purposes, in the belief that

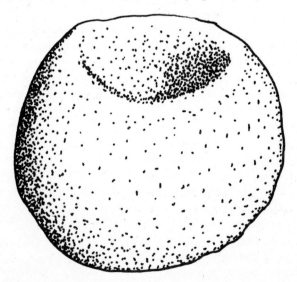

Basaltic lava mortar from Yana territory, about ten inches high.

these had been made by Coyote. However, Maidu families cherished portable stone mortars. They were kept buried at some distance from the dwelling, and dug up for occasional inspection. Bed-rock acorn pounding holes are not found in this region either except for the Maidu area. Instead, acorn meats were placed in hopper baskets lacking bottoms. This basketry mortar hopper rested with the small open end down on a heavy flat stone. The pounding basket was held in place by the Indian woman's knees as she sat in front of and straddling it. In one hand she wielded a stone pestle, flat on the grinding end. With the other hand she stirred the acorn material so that the coarse pieces worked toward the center to get the full impact of the pounding. The hopper basket was not always used, by the mountain Maidu, the pounding often being done merely on a flat rock slab, the woman's free hand continually brushing the acorn material back to the center. Acorn meal was ground until it was as fine as flour. The coarse pieces were separated from the fine by a process which employed a flattish piece of wood or bark a foot or so across. Sometimes a basketry plaque was used. A portion of ground meal was placed on this tray which was held firmly at one side and inclined toward the operator. The other edge of the plaque was shaken, causing the coarse material to roll into a container held in the lap for repounding while the fine flour remained on the plaque. A small brush, generally made from the pounded and dried root of the soap-plant, was used to brush the flour off and into the cooking basket. Mountain Maidu, according to Voegelin, actually did sift acorn meal through open-work baskets though this was not a common practice even among members of this tribe.

White oak and some other acorn flour could be used for cooking without further preparation. Atsugewi preferred black oak acorns which had to be leached to remove the bitter tannic acid before using. To do this the flour was placed in a shallow depression on clean sand over porous earth, usually, but Yana used loosely woven baskets for the purpose, and in recent times it has become common practice to place cloth flour sacking over a screen or sieve. Cold water was poured over the meal until it was nearly free of bitterness. Warm water was then employed briefly, but hot water was never used, for it would make the flour tend to jell. Sand was removed from the bottom of the flour by touching the bottom of a handful of the moist material to water. The flour held together, but the sand grains dropped off. The flour could be dried and stored at this point, but was usually used as it was prepared.

Portions of about two or three quarts of acorn flour were placed in cooking baskets a foot or more in diameter. Water was added and then hot stones were dropped in. These smoothly rounded stones, of any shape and from one and a half to three inches in diameter, had been heated in an open fire. They were quickly dipped into water to remove ashes before being put into the mush cooking basket. The method of handling these cooking stones seems to have varied. Present day Atsugewi say a small looped stick was used, but old informants stated that two forked sticks were employed. Stirring had to be continuous lest the cooking stones scorch the basket. Atsugewi used any convenient stick for this, but Yana had a small oak paddle. After boiling a short while the acorn mush became light greyish or brownish in color; when cooled it jellied quite firmly. Acorn mush was commonly eaten warm with meat, from small individual baskets. Spoons were unknown in the Lassen area so acorn mush was eaten with index and second fingers, Mountain Maidu made their acorn mush of a more liquid consistency so that it was often consumed by drinking.

Acorn bread was made by using less water and adding a small amount of reddish iron-bearing or blackish salt-bearing soil by Atsugewi, but mountain Maidu left this ingredient out. The paste was molded into biscuit or loaf-shaped forms, wrapped in leaves and baked all night in earth pit ovens. Yana sometimes added red soil to their acorn bread making it brightly colored. Usually black oak acorns were used for bread by the Yana tribes and white oak for soup.

That acorns are a fine food is indicated by the following analysis of the uncooked meal. The proportions vary somewhat, but not importantly among the several kinds of acorns used: 21% fat, 5% protein, 62% carbohydrate, and 14% water, mineral, and fiber. In cooked acorn mush the proportions remain the same relatively, except, of course, for the greatly increased water content.

Buckeye nuts, not used much by Atsugewi, were important to other Indians of California, especially those residing at lower elevations. These fruits were gathered when ripe, then shelled, pounded and soaked in loosely woven baskets until the poisonous juice was leached out. The pulpy mass was next squeezed to remove excess water. Unlike acorn meal buckeye pulp was eaten uncooked. Yana crushed their buckeyes with their feet and leached the material in creeks, though sometimes hot water was used.

Nuts of digger pine and sugar pine were highly regarded as food. Men climbed trees and picked digger pine cones or shook limbs to dislodge sugar pine cones.   The cones were placed on end and covered with dry grass which was burned, ridding the cones of pitch.   After this heat treatment, sugar pine nuts came out easily when cone scales were p u l l e d back.   After singeing the heavy digger pine cones were hit with rocks to obtain the large nuts they contained.

The white sweet crusty deposit occasionally found on the bark of sugar pines was relished as candy by Atsugewi. However, it had a laxative property which mountain Maidu recognized and reputedly employed as such.

A variety of small plant seeds also provided tasty nutrition. Several members of the sunflower family including balsam root species and mules ears, and others were used by all local tribes. Such seeds were usually collected by beating them with paddle-shaped basketry seed beaters into burden baskets.   They were then parched with coals in flat trays, placed in flat baskets and worked about with stones until freed of skins.   Seeds were winnowed by tossing them up allowing wind to carry hulls and skins away.   The seeds were then pulverized with a small stone or muller, being rolled or rubbed on a larger rock slab generally referred to as a metate.   Such seeds were eaten dry by Atsugewi, Yana, and Yahi without grinding, or the flour might be moistened and molded into cakes about the size of biscuits and eaten without further cooking. However, Yana also cooked certain sunflower seeds and the yellow blossoming heads of the small *(Helianthella)* sunflower were themselves cooked and eaten.

Clover tops were collected in summer and eaten fresh by all local tribes. Mountain Maidu also baked them in earth pit ovens, then dried and stored the m a t e r i a l to be recooked in winter for making soup. Atsugewi cooked clover roots in ovens. Young thistle stalks were eaten raw as was the foliage of several carrot-like plants. Mushrooms, fresh, roasted, or dried were eaten also. Young soap-plant stems were eaten fresh or baked and dried for winter use by Yana tribes.

Manzanita berries were gathered by all Indians of the Lassen region in July and August. These berries were knocked into burden baskets with a stick.   They were dried, stored in pits, pounded when needed, and sifted as fine meal.   This was moistened and molded into biscuit-sized cakes and put away until wanted. Either fresh flour or the cakes were e a t e n plain or put into water and drunk.   One investigator reported fermentation of manzanita cider and its use as a mild intoxicant, but this appears to have been the exception rather than the rule.   The drink, of lemonade-like character, was usually consumed fresh. Manzanita cider was conveyed to the mouth by dipping a deer tail sop into the liquid, and then by sucking it. Small cakes were made of a mixture of manzanita and wild plum flours. Yana and Yahi also ate manzanita berries as such either fresh, or roasted and dried.

Red berries of skunk or squaw bush were gathered in midsummer, washed, dried, and stored. They were pounded into flour in a mortar basket, mixed with manzanita flour and drunk. Elderberries were mashed and mixed with manzanita flour and stored as cakes.

Wild plums were prepared by removing seeds. These were then eaten fresh or dried for storage.

Chokecherries and service berries were put into baskets when ripe and mashed. The paste was eaten without cooking.

Gooseberries, huckleberries, currants, Oregon-grape, buckthorn, juniper, thimble, and elderberries were eaten fresh, too, but juniper fruits might be dried and pounded into flour and stored.

Another item used as food was salt which mountain Maidu and Yana gathered locally in mineral form. The Atsugewi also imported it from Round Mountain in North Yana territory or made expeditions to this site to gather the dark salt material from a certain marsh. This salty earth was shaped into black loaves and dried. It was not only used for flavoring, but the black soil was also eaten as such by some individuals. Atsugewi had a local source of salt, however, by collecting fine whitish crystals in the early mornings from the blades of salt grass which was run between the fingers. Atsugewi used salt for salmon and venison in cooking, but not in drying processes.

Pine pitch was chewed, but Atsugewi also used milkweed chewing gum.

As for eating customs, Atsugewi ate three meals each day. Mountain Maidu just prepared two real meals. Hands were washed after eating deer and bear meats. Mountain Maidu wiped faces and hands with bark and grass after eating.

There was a well defined division of labor among California Indians. Men would carry water for unusually long distances or heavy logs for firewood, but women usually carried water, wood, acorn and root crops, and the like. In the case of moving camp, however, men carried the heaviest burdens. The most important division of labor was the delegation to men of all activities concerning animals and animal products, and to women all pertaining to vegetable materials. Women, for instance, collected materials for basketry and made all the baskets, except that men often made basketry fish traps and nets. Women dug roots and cooked all food except meat which men normally cooked. Exception to this rule was necessarily made when men were away on hunting trips or at war. Men usually built the houses, made moccasins and skin clothing too.

Among Atsugewi and mountain Maidu only men made fire, but this was accomplished by both sexes among the Yana and Yahi.

CHAPTER IX
HOUSES AND FURNISHINGS

The Atsugewi used earth-covered lodges as their permanent winter dwellings. These varied in size from about nine feet in length, for a single family, to more than thirty feet in length for a chief's house which was usually larger than other houses. Most frequently houses were about twenty feet long and somewhat narrower, being occupied by three to five families. The earth lodge was elliptical in shape with one center post planted firmly in the earth floor somewhat back of true center. This supported beams running to two smaller secondary posts and to earth shoulders which resulted from excavation of the entire floor to a depth of about three feet. On the beams other poles or rafters and bark slabs (usually of incense-cedar) were laid. The whole sloping roof was then covered with pine needles and a layer of earth.

The main entrance was through a hole about in the center of the roof. Over this a heavy mat was placed in bad weather. This opening also served as a smoke hole. A ladder made of two poles with cross pieces tied on with serviceberry withes was used inside.

A secondary entrance of small size, used by children, was built

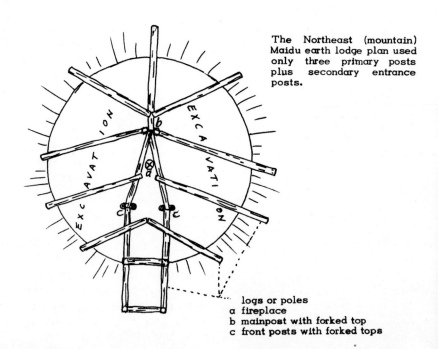

The Northeast (mountain) Maidu earth lodge plan used only three primary posts plus secondary entrance posts.

logs or poles
a fireplace
b mainpost with forked top
c front posts with forked tops

horizontally at ground level on the south (front) end of the house. It projected tunnel-like a short distance beyond the lodge outside wall. The main purpose of this ground level opening was to act as a ventilator duct to supply draft for proper burning of the cooking and house warming fire which burned in front of the center post. At night the ventilator duct was closed. This reduced air supply, causing the fire to burn very slowly. Glowing coals developed as a result. These produced reduced but adequate heat for the occupants who slept with their feet to the fire. Men did all of the house construction work except for excavation. The women did this with digging sticks and wooden or basketry scoops with which they threw the dirt out of the pit. Excavation of the floor of the lodge not only made it easier to construct a strong house, but contributed materially to the warmth of the standard winter house.

Typical winter house of the local permanent Indian villages at lower elevations.

There was no furniture as such. Each family used an assigned portion of the house, and cooked its own food, but utilized the central communal fire. A thin layer of grass, carefully kept away from the fire, covered the floor. The Indians slept on the floor on mats made of tule. During the day these and the sleeping blankets were rolled up and provided the only seats. However, sitting usually consisted of squatting on the floor.

Blankets of deer and elk skin were generally used. Atsugewi also used loose tule or grass blankets and all our tribes employed both woven rabbit skin and patchwork rabbit or fox blankets. Yana in addition to all the foregoing utilized bear skins; sometimes they removed the hair from their blankets.

Atsugewi pillows were of bundles of leaves or grass while those of the mountain Maidu were harder, being merely piles of small poles, blocks of wood, or rocks.

Interior earth walls of the houses were sometimes hung with tule mats or skins fastened with pegs to prevent dirt from sloughing off and rolling onto the floor. A few shelves might also be provided by laying wooden slabs on sticks driven into the dirt walls.

There were other less substantial winter houses consisting either of small double lean-tos of bark slabs or conical houses on frameworks of slender poles and with shallow excavations. Some dirt was thrown against the outside walls for added warmth. Lazy people, who were usually consequently poor in the necessities and comforts of normal Indian life, lived in this more flimsy type of house. Also, women when indisposed repaired to such huts. A doorway was left in the siding to be closed by a tule mat in these little houses. They were also equipped with small smoke holes

Atsugewi bark house

for central fires.

Atsugewi summer houses as such really did not exist. Summer camps were little more than circular enclosures of brush, juniper, or other conifer limbs or of rock. These were ten or fifteen feet across with openings to the east. There was no roof, although branches and bark slabs might be put over crude frames in rainy weather. If a person were caught in a sudden shower he might make a temporary shelter by leaning bark slabs, if available, against a large rock or log lying on the ground.

Atsugewi did not have any separate sweat houses nor dancing or assembly chambers, but used the larger earth lodge houses for these purposes. The largest belonged to chiefs and to other well-to-do Indians. Heat for sweating was provided directly by fire and not by production of steam as was the case with Plains Indians who threw water on hot stones. In recent years, however, after introduction of the horse, Atsugewi learned the latter technique and also constructed Plains Indian type sweat houses of one to three person capacity. These were dome shaped, and built of willow poles set in the ground in a circle. The tops were bent over and tied down, and this framework was covered with skins.

Old type sweating was for men only, but Indian women---usually wives---also sweated with men in the new style separate sweat houses. Old time Atsugewi purposes in sweating were for gaining success in hunting, in gambling, and for general good luck. Some praying was done, but there were no formalized ceremonies or dances amongst the Atsugewi. Men sometimes slept in sweat houses.

In the case of all local tribes sweating was followed by a cold plunge, if available nearby. Lacking this facility, a cold sponge bath was taken.

The mountain Maidu earth lodge for dwelling and sweating was similar to that of the Atsugewi. However, northeast Maidu earth lodges "koom" were simpler and smaller than those of northwest and southern Maidu. Three posts, often forked were used in place of 10 or 11 employed for valley lodges. Excavation was about three feet deep, circular in plan, and from 18 to 40 feet across. A large flat stone was placed upright at the foot of the mainpost between it and the fire in the center. The vertical walls of the excavation were usually covered or lined with vertically placed whole or split logs or with bark slabs. Logs were lain horizontally on the three posts as indicated on the accompanying sketch. Radial rafters supporting the roof were placed on these beams and sloping downward to the ground surface outside as well as to two small posts at the small openway or ventilator passage. Cross poles were placed horizontally on the rafters and on these, large pieces of bark, branches, and pine needles were successively laid. Lastly, a heavy covering of soil 8 to 20 inches thick was heaped on the structure. On top in the center a smokehole was left, large enough to serve as the main entrance originally, but after the coming of white man, the smokehole was made smaller, and, instead, the originally small ventilator tunnel which sloped from floor level up to the ground surface outside was enlarged, thus supplanting the smokehole as the main entrance. Originally a ladder of two poles with cross pieces tied on with grapevine or other wythes gave vertical access from the floor to the smokehole entrance. Dixon reports that a notched log was sometimes used for the purpose among mountain Maidu.

The koom or lodge was occupied from November to March and was situated on the edges of wide meadows in mountain Maidu areas. At lower elevation occupancy was more or less continous.

Mountain Maidu did not have separate sweat houses. They always used a large earth dwelling lodge for the purpose. This was similar to the Atsugewi practice. These Maidu did, however, have a formalized sweat dance. Also different from the Atsugewi was the practice of men using the sweat house for gambling, handicraft work, and competitive singing.

The "hoe-bow" of the mountain Maidu was a hut, 8 to 15 feet in diameter and excavated 12 to 15 inches deep. Two main poles were securely tied near the end. From the resulting "V" at the top, shorter poles were laid to a pair of slender posts about three feet high and set about three feet apart along the edge of the excavation. Against this frame branches, bark, and leaves were piled and earth was heaped around the bottom. The doors of all such bark huts opened to the south and were hung with a skin or tule mat.

The rude summer shelter or shade provider was just like that of the Atsugewi.

Information on Yahi house details are somewhat scanty, but in all probability they were small conical bark-covered huts while some larger earth lodges were built to house several families --- in general similar, but perhaps smaller than those of the other tribes of the Lassen area. The large pretentious lodge, constructed solely for sweating and ceremonies, of the Sacramento Valley tribes seems to have been lacking among all of our local tribes.

The common bark hut dwelling of the Yana was apparently built over a circular depression two feet deep, the top of the house rising about six feet above the ground. It was probably like the mountain Maidu huts, being a series of poles resting on the edges of the excavation. These met and were tied at the top to form a cone of low slope, although some informants claimed that the posts were set so firmly that tying together was omitted. The frames were covered with pine and incense-cedar bark slabs leaving a smoke hole near each apex. Earth was probably banked on the lower sloping walls. Entrance was never through the smoke hole as in the case of Atsugewi and some mountain Maidu earth lodge houses, but by means of a small door at ground level on the south side. The entrance was protected by a little covered way extending outward three feet from the house wall, and decked over by a gable roof of low pitch. A ramp of low pitch extended from the floor of the house through this antechamber to the ground level outside as no steps were constructed.

The Yana lodge houses were not numerous. The ground plan was long, usually wedge or oval in outline and designed for several families, each with its own fire. As with the other tribes discussed in this booklet, such buildings also served as sweat houses. A ladder consisting of a notched log extended down from the smoke hole to the floor. One, two, or three center posts with radiating rafters and shorter side posts were employed. The Yana followed the Atsugewi practice of providing each earth lodge with a south facing, ground level, tunnel-like ventilator entrance of small size. It is possible that Yana did have a few special sweating lodges of the same design, but the matter is debatable. During sweating Yana men talked and played; the main purpose of sweating was to make men strong.

It has already been pointed out that all four tribes which used what is now Lassen Volcanic National Park did so only during the summer. During their high mountain sojourn, the local Indians did not live in houses as such. There, residence during the three or four summer months was in temporary camps, usually roofless circular areas to accomodate several families. These were fenced in with brush and were entered by one or more openings somewhat in the same manner as campsites reserved for visitors at their permanent villages at lower elevations. Four-posted horizontal roofs, to provide shade, were sometimes constructed too. Yana seem to have made a lean-to or hut with grass and bark covering for summer roofs.

Chapter X

HOUSEHOLD TOOLS, IMPLEMENTS, AND WEAPONS

Implements for grinding foods were important. Mountain Maidu, in fact all Maidu tribes, ground some acorns on flat bed rock. When the resultant holes which eventually developed in the rock surfaces became deep, they were abandoned as the acorn meal tended to pack into hard lumps at the bottoms there of. A heavy flat stone grinding slab was most frequently used. However, all Lassen area tribes had portable stone mortar bowls too. The Atsugewi and mountain Maidu did not make these nor did they use them for grinding food. Such portable stone mortars were found, evidently having been fashioned by more ancient tribes. Supernatural powers were ascribed to these mortars, and they were used only by shamans or medicine men. The Maidu thought that stone mortar bowls were made by Coyote at the time of creation and scattered over the world for the use of mankind. Others believed the mortars to have been "first people" originally, who were turned to stones in this form upon the coming of the Indian people at which time other "first people" were transformed into animals.

As has been described under the preparation of acorn mush, local tribes used the flat stone pounding slab under an open bottomed hopper basket, most commonly. The hopper basket of the Atsugewi and mountain Maidu was usually of twined construction and bound often with buckskin about the basal edge. Mountain Maidu sometimes employed their coiling technique in making the acorn pounding basket. It was from this tribe, at the turn of the

Northeast Maidu soapstone bowl
six inches wide — a rare article (after Dixon)

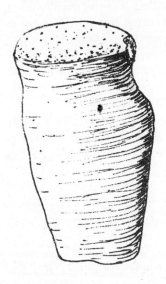

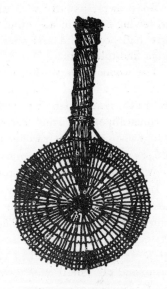

Maidu stone axe head,
5 inches long (after Dixon)

One of several seed
beater types used locally

century, that Atsugewi learned to make their pounding hopper
baskets of the stronger coiled construction.

Pestles of stone were long, smoothed, and sometimes flattened
on the sides. This resulted from use of these implements also as
rubbing or mulling stones for processing small seeds on flat slabs
without employment of basket hoppers. The pestles were always
without the ornamentation used by certain other California tribes.
The pounding end of the food grinding pestles are ever so slightly
convex---their grinding surfaces are nearly flat. This is in contrast to pestles used in the deep bowl-shaped portable stone
mortars for ceremonial purposes. The grinding ends of these pestles
were strongly rounded, nearly hemispherical in shape.

The muller or small seed crusher used on the flat grinding slab
without a hopper basket was of oval or rectangular shape, and it
too was unornamented.

Small brushes used in miscellaneous food preparation were made
of pounded dried soap-plant bulb fibers.

Hot rocks for cooking were usually handled with two sticks.
None of our tribes used spoons. Crude obsidian knives with, or
more commonly without, bone handles were used for many chores.

Yana used split cobble stones for cutting and scraping operations. Their stone knives sometimes had wrapped buckskin handles.

Bone awls, usually with wrapped handles, were commonly used for sewing buckskin and other hides. Atsugewi are said by some to have had both eyed and open notched needles of bone for sewing skins and tule mats.

The wooden shuttle for net weaving was a stick notched at both ends and was used by all of the local tribes. A squarish wooden net mesh spacer permitted nets to be properly made.

Mountain Maidu used deer antler wedges for splitting wood while Atsugewi used wooden wedges---especially of mountain-mahogany. Wedges were usually driven with simple wooden clubs, though rocks might be employed for the purpose.

Drills for boring holes in shell work and for making pipes and the like were used by Atsugewi only. Such drills were wooden shafts with stone points. These were rotated by rolling the shaft between the palms of the hands. Where the drill was not in use, holes were made in pieces of wood with live coals. Sometimes unfinished clamshell money was received in trade perhaps at a discount. Such pieces were strung tightly onto a cord and the whole string was then rolled between two flat stones thus grinding the shell edges to make the well formed disks characteristic of clam shell money.

Fire making drills were of greater importance. All local tribes employed them. Those of this area were one-piece hand rotated

Soap-root fiber acorn meal brush about 6 inches long (after Dixon)

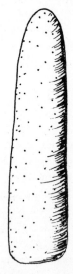

A lava pestle, flat ended food pounder, about 10 inches long

Maidu bone awls or basket "needles"
about 6 inches long

affairs which did not utilize the labor saving drill bow of the mid-
west. A long buckeye wood stick about half an inch thick was
twirled on a notched block of incense-cedar or juniper wood. A
bed of dry shredded grass and incense-cedar or other flamable
tinder was used to nourish the spark into flame. Both sexes made
fire among the Yana and Yahi, but unless the men were away,
Atsugewi and mountain Maidu women did not make fire. Buckeye
was uncommon or lacking in the areas of the latter tribes, so this
material had to be traded from the Yana and Yahi. Buckeye fire
making sticks commanded quite a price, a piece two feet long often
selling for ten completed arrows. Since fire making required much
effort and skill, fire was rarely allowed to go out. A "slow match"
consisting of a piece of punky wood in which the fire smouldered
was usually carried along.

It was as true in prehistoric America as it is today that weapons
were essential to existence. Weapons were necessary not only for
warfare---whether aggressive or defensive---but for the securing
of game for food since domestication of animals was not practiced.

The bow and arrow was the only important weapon of California
Indians. Local bows were rather short and quite broad in cross-
section. We quote Garth's "Atsugewi Ethnography" on the subject
as follows:

".... The best bows were made by the Atsuge, who had a supply of yew wood .... along the western borders of their territory. The Paiute were anxious to trade for Atsuge bows and considered them much superior to their own. In making the bow a piece of yew wood was selected, split, and shaved down with flints and pumice stone to the required form and thickness. After it had been wrapped in green grass and roasted in hot ashes, the bow was bent to required shape (recurved tips with a slight incurve at the middle), which it retained when it cooled off. Sinew, taken from the back of a deer, was softened by chewing and was then glued on the back of the bow in short strips, which were rubbed out as flat as possible with a smooth piece of bone. Salmon skins were boiled to make the glue.

"The designs painted in green and red on the backs of

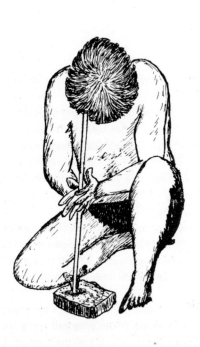

Yahi making fire by twirling buckeye rod on Incense-cedar block

Maidu fire drill of buckeye (right) about 28 inches long. In the two inch wide Incense-cedar slab note the cut notches with a deeper twirling hole at the head of each

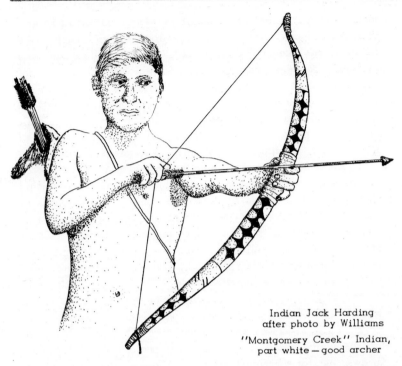

Indian Jack Harding
after photo by Williams

"Montgomery Creek" Indian,
part white — good archer

An Atsugewi type bow characteristically short, broad, sinew backed
and held at 45 degree angle in shooting. Note the painted decoration

bows are among the few examples of masculine art. The painting was done with a feather tip. The sinew for the bowstring
. . . . was chewed to make it soft and then it was made into a
two-ply cord by rolling it with the open hand on the thigh.
After salmon glue was rubbed in to make the fibers stick together, the string was stretched by tying a rock to one end and
allowing it to hang down from some support. A tassel . . . . of
mole skin might be attached to the end of the bow for decoration . . . .

" . . . . Flint tipped arrows . . . . were made of cane or rose
and had foreshafts of Serviceberry, or they might be entirely of
Service wood. Cane arrows . . . . with a sharp-pointed foreshaft of Serviceberry were commonly used for small animals
and birds. Such arrows might be unfeathered . . . . (an informant) recalled a bird arrow . . . . with a barbed wooden point.
Deer-bone pointed arrows were sometimes used for killing
deer and other game. Voegelin reports that these arrows were
also sometimes barbed. Flint-tipped arrows were about thirty

inches long. . . . arrows for small game were somewhat shorter than flint-tipped arrows . . . . the wood was ordinarily dried before it was used. The end of the Serviceberry foreshaft was cut into a dowel which was inserted in the soft pithy center of the main shaft, the juncture being wrapped with sinew. A notch one-fourth of an inch deep was cut in the butt. A laterally notched obsidian arrow point was inserted in the split end of the foreshaft and bound on with cross lashings of sinew. The binding was ordinarily waterproofed with pitch.

"Two small grooved pumice stones were used to smooth arrow shafts. The foreshaft was painted red as an indication that poison had been applied to the point. Other bands or stripes of color toward the nock end of the arrow served as ownership marks . . . . the stripes might run spirally as on a stick of candy . . . . all kinds of colors being used for painting arrows. Feathers were split along the midrib and were glued to the shaft, about a finger's width below the butt, with pitch. Sinew wrapping bound down each end of the feathers, three of which --- about four inches long --- were used to an arrow. The edge of the feather was burned smooth with a hot coal. Feathers of hawks or similar birds were used on ordinary arrows, but for the finest arrows---those to be used for bear and deer---eagle feathers were employed. An arrow wrench of bone or wood was used for straightening arrows; or they might simply be straightened by using the teeth as a vise. A flat antelope horn might be perforated and used as an arrow wrench . . . . (John La Mar) had a small triangular stone with a hole in the center . . . . which, he said was heated in the fire and used for straightening cane arrows.

"Although the flint points themselves were considered

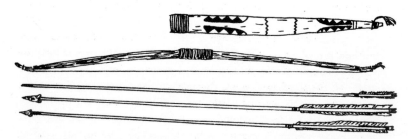

Maidu bow 40 inches long and two inches wide, deer sinew backed and painted with powdered greenish rock from Oregon mixed with Salmon glue Two arrows are obsidian tipped. (after Dixon)

Painted Atsugewi bows (after Garth)

a. Goose Valley, design in red (Apwaruge)
b. Goose Valley, design in red (Apwaruge)
c. Drawn by Dave Brown (Atsuge) with
   outer lines red, inner lines green

poisonous, an arrow poison was often used for larger game
as well as in war. The usual method of making poison was
to take the liver or pancreas of a deer and allow it to rot;
the material was then smeared on the arrow point. . . ."
Rattlesnake poison was also employed; however none of the
poisoned arrow concoctions were very effective except to start
infection of wounds inflicted by arrowpoints so treated.

Arrow points found in the park area, in the territory of both
Atsugewi and mountain Maidu are most frequently of obsidian, but
sometimes are of a dense dull black basalt lava. The term flint
is a very loose one, being applied to obsidian, chert, opal, chalcedony, and even to the dense basalt, noted above, in common usage.

Mountain Maidu imported yew wood as this did not commonly
grow in their own territory. This tribe, however, also manufactured
its own bows. In practically all respects bow and arrow design and
execution were identical to that of the Atsugewi. Those of Yana
and Yahi were similar too. All tribes of the Lassen area fashioned
arrow points with barbs. In addition mountain Maidu flaked points
without barbs but with basal stems for attachment were made.

The bow was most frequently held in shooting at an angle of
about 45 degrees with the arrow on top. Mountain Maidu used that
style, too, or else held the bow horizontally with the arrow on top
except in case of war when the arrow was held on the underside of

Dull black obsidian much more convex on one side than on the other. From near Corral Meadow; one and one half inches.

Black obsidian near Little Willow Lake; one and one half inches long.

Dense black basalt from Terminal Geyser; one and five eights inches

Black obsidian near Little Willow Lake, one inch long.

MOUNTAIN MAIDU STONE POINTS

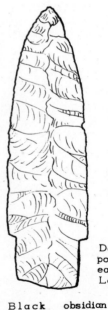

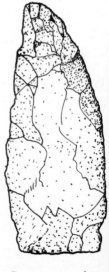

Dark gray banded point from Northeast shore Snag Lake; two inches.

Dark gray obsidian point from Battle Creek Meadows. Note unusually strong asymmetry in two planes; one inch long.

Black obsidian spear point or knife from south shore of Summit Lake; four inches.

Coarse gray lava knife (?) from Battle Creek Meadows; Three and one half inches long.

ATSUGEWI KNIFE (?) AND
ARROW POINT

SOUTHERN YANA POINTS

Maidu bone arrow point flaker about ten inches long (after Dixon)

the bow. Gifford and Klimak reveal that northern and central Yana held the bow horizontally. Sapir and Spier found that the Yana tribes proper (not Yahi), however held bows vertically in shooting. All tribes considered except Yahi used the primary release of the arrow in shooting. In this method the arrow was held between the index and third fingers, which caught and pulled back the string. The thumb held the other side of the arrow. The Yahi, on the other hand used the Mongolian release; grasping the arrow with the thumb and unbent first joints of the first and second fingers.

". . . . the arrow was let fly between the index and third finger of the left hand, which held the bow. Many arrow points were uniface and curved slightly to one side. . . . . A hunter, when shooting at a distant object, turned the arrow so that the point curved up; when shooting an object close by, he turned the arrow so that the point curved down. A hunter carried at least one arrow in his left hand with his bow. Extra arrows were carried in a quiver . . . . (made of) coyote, raccoon, or other skins. Ordinarily the hunter carried his quiver on his back, but if he wanted to be able to reach the arrows easily, he hung it on his . . . . shoulder so that it fell under his left armpit. Arrows were taken from the quiver with the right hand." Inside the quiver, at the bottom, a cushion of dry grass was placed to prevent the stone points from chipping each other.

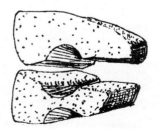

Maidu arrow — straightener and smoother of sandstone about three inches long (after Dixon)

Nearly colorless obsidian south of Sulphur Works; three quarters inch.

Off-white chalcedony point south of Sulphur Works area; one and one half inches.

Black obsidian one and one quarter inches long and a full one half inch thick.

Three inch point of coarse gray lava from Mill Creek Canyon.

Black obsidian. South of Sulphur Works, one and one half inches.

YAHI STONE POINTS

Yana arrow points one and one half to two inches long. The materials used are mostly black obsidian, also dark grey and buff obsidian. One is of dense black basalt.

A pair of Yana arrow smoother and straightening stones made of porous glassy (pre-Lassen?) dacite pumice, length about two and one half inches

War clubs were not used. Atsugewi claim to have had a stone axe, sharpened by chipping and lashed with sinew to a split oak or mountain-mahogany handle a foot or so long. It was used for chopping roots and small trees on occasion, but the stone axe was certainly not widely used by California Indians, and even among Atsugewi it may have been unknown until the coming of white man, or knowledge of it may have been gained from Plains Indians after the advent of the horse. The tomahawk, so important to Indians of eastern and midwestern North America, was unknown to California Indians. Trees were normally felled and cut by controlled burning.

Four-foot spears, tipped with large flaked stone points for fighting at close quarters, were used by all local tribes on occasion, but were not numerous. Only the Yana are believed to have thrown the weapon; the more common usage seems to have been by energetically thrusting it.

Knives or daggers as fighting implements were made of chipped obsidian but were quite rare. A short, crude, one edged, stone knife was used widely as a general utility implement, but not in combat nor in killing game. Yana Indians also employed a mussel shell knife for light delicate work around camp. Atsugewi and mountain Maidu sometimes affixed wooden handles to their obsidian knives. These two tribes also fashioned knives of sharpened bone and horn.

Of equipment for warfare, Garth states:

"Defensive armor included rod armor . . . . , gowns . . . . of dried elk or bear skins, and skin helmets which came down

A wooden arrow straightener from northern California (Yurok)

Atsugewi stone arrow—straightener

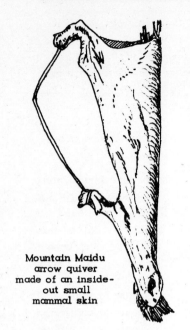

Mountain Maidu
arrow quiver
made of an inside-
out small
mammal skin

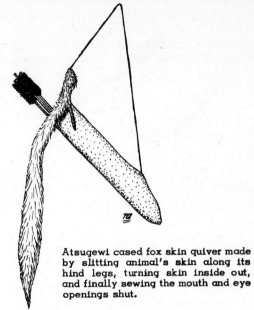

Atsugewi cased fox skin quiver made
by slitting animal's skin along its
hind legs, turning skin inside out,
and finally sewing the mouth and eye
openings shut.

4½ inches   7 inches
Maidu stone knives of obsidian,
one with a wooden and sinew handle
(after Dixon)

A warrior in stick armor
and fur helmet

over the forehead and ears, 'so a man could just see out of it'. The skin armor extended to the ankles or lower; it was worn over one shoulder so that it protected only the side of the body turned toward the enemy.   Rod armor, made of serviceberry withes twined together with buckskin string, was high enough to come up to the neck under the chin and extended two or three inches below the belt. The Plains Indian shield, although found among the Surprise Valley Paiute and other Paiute tribes to the east, was lacking among the Atsugewi,'' and all other tribes of the Lassen area.

Chapter XI
BASKETRY AND TEXTILES

The outstanding art of the Indians of California was their basketry. In fact the excellence of California basketry generally is not exceeded elsewhere in North America. Size varies from that of a pea to that of a bushel basket. Both weave and ornamentation were very diversified.

Basketry of the Lassen area, especially that of the Atsugewi and mountain Maidu, was of good quality. Both coiled and twined types of basketry (to be described below) were made by mountain Maidu, but the Atsugewi did not learn the art of coiled basketry from the Maidu until the early 1900's. Yana and Yahi wove both types but twined baskets were by far the more numerous. This is due to the fact that these tribes were akin to the twining tribes of the north. Close contact with the neighboring Wintun tribes of the Sacramento Valley resulted in the addition of limited amount of coiling technique in their basketry making over the years.

Coiled basketry itself had some technical variations with which we shall not concern ourselves. The coiling technique was characteristic of the central and southern part of the California area. Mountain Maidu used three willow rods in a parallel group which ran as a core in a continous spiral starting at the center of the basket. This was the warp element. The bundle of three willow ribs was lashed to the preceding basketry by a strand or weft (filler) of the inner bark of redbud. This was accomplished by poking an awl through the preceding row, and separating the stitches. In

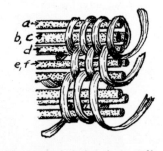

Technique of the three willow rod (or rib) coiled basketry (after Otis T. Mason). Note that the lashing strand anchors the three new ribs "a" "b", and "c" to the top rib "d" of the preceding three "d", "e", and "f" group

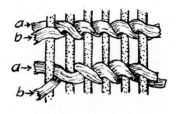

Simple twined basketry technique employs two weft (lashing) strands, but when overlaying with another material is done two or more layers will make up each of the strands "a" and "b" (modified from Otis T. Mason)

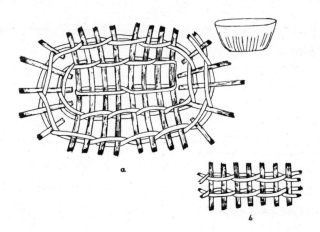

Variations of the simple twined basketry technique: a. method of starting the round root-cleaning basket; b, detail of side wall of basket showing open work weave. (Garth)

doing so, the awl was passed under the topmost of the core or warp of three coiling willow ribs. A Redbud bark strand was then slipped through the awl hole, thus lashing the three loose willow ribs down by passing the strand around them and through the next awl hole in the preceding row. Recent Atsugewi coiled basketry technique is similar in all details, having been learned from the Maidu.

Twined basketry consisted of willow ribs radiating from a common center. These twigs were the warp. The weft of filling and binding stitches were split pine root strands. Dixon states that mountain Maidu sometimes dyed pine root black by burying it in mud mixed with charcoal. Pine root was tightly woven in to make the bottom of the basket which was normally undecorated. More and more willow ribs were added as the basket became larger. The willow ribs were curved up when willow rib additions were decreased. As the sides began to be built up on these twined baskets, each pine root stitch, both inside and outside, was covered with a whitish strand of bear-grass or squaw-grass. The tops of baskets were often left unfinished after the unused willow warps were clipped off. The basket did not unravel in use. However, the best baskets were finished by adding a marginal strengthening ring of choke cherry or willow which was bound to the basket body firmly and neatly, usually by wrapping with strands of redbud bark. During weaving willow withes were fastened inside of the basket to help it retain its shape, but these were removed upon completion of the basket.

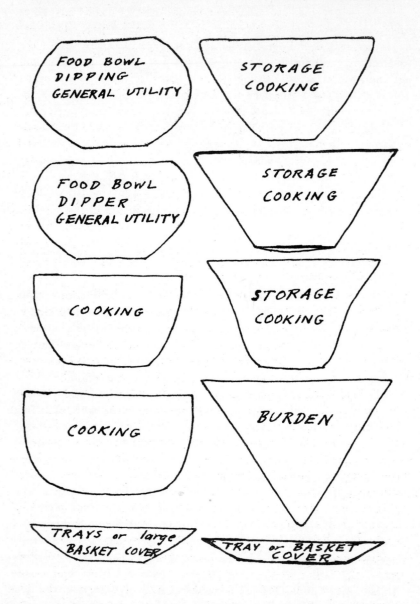

Side outline shapes of Maidu baskets (after Dixon). The plan of virtually all Maidu baskets was circular. Twined storage baskets are up to three feet in diameter for holding seed, meal, etc. Open twined construction was used for storage of whole acorns, fish, and meat. Flatish circular basketry plaque was for "vibration sifting".

Some utility baskets were undecorated, being made merely of pine root and willow, or, if coiled, of redbud and willow. However, most baskets bore some designs. They were all named and were inspired by the objects of nature about these outdoor peoples, and not the product of their imaginations. Nevertheless, the designs are quite stylized, often to the extent that recognition of the inspiration is difficult or impossible.

In the case of twined baskets the designs were made by substituting outer redbud bark for squaw-grass to produce a dull red instead of the white overlaid stitches of the rest of the basket. As a result of the double twining technique the designs were seen equally well on the inside and the outside of each basket. Black designs were of overlaid maidenhair fern *(Adiantum pedatum)* stems. However, mountain Maidu also used common bracken fern *(Pteris aquilinum)* for black designs. Indians to the north of the Atsugewi used roots and stems of certain sedges treated with charcoal and mud or with ashes and water to produce basketry materials of black and of warm henna-brown coloration respectively. These were used on occasion by Atsugewi. The bear-grass, redbud, and maidenhair fern decorative materials were most commonly used by all tribes of this area. Atsugewi are the only local Indians to have used feathers to adorn their baskets. They used the shiny iridescent blue-green feathers from the necks of male mallard ducks. This was not common, however, and by no means used as often nor developed to the fine art and diversity of the famous Pomo feathered basketry of the Clear Lake region of the California Coast Range. Atsugewi are also believed to have occasionally adorned some basketry work with shell beads and porcupine quills, but this must have been quite rare or more examples would have survived to the present day.

Outer bark of redbud almost always decorated coiled baskets.

Concerning Maidu basketry Dixon states that the vast majority of the articles are of the coiled type, twining technique being used only for burden baskets and hopper or grinding baskets. For the radial ribs of the former they used shoots of hazel *(Corylus rostrata* var. *californica)* when available. He points out too, the frequent use of the feather, quail-tip, and arrow-point designs not only among the mountain Maidu, but among all Maidu. A characteristic of this group of Indians also, in contrast to other local tribes, is the tendency to confine one design to a basket rather than combining designs. Maidu employed a wide variety of designs. Many of them represent animals and plants. A considerable number

Atsugewi basket, twined and overlaid with bear-grass and maiden hair fern.

Atsugewi general utility basket of twined construction with lizard foot design. Underside shown to reveal dark (actually tan-colored) area of bare split pine root weft without bear-grass or maiden hair overlay.

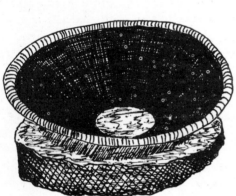

Maidu hopper, pounding, or milling basket of twined construction on rock mortar slab. Diameter about eighteen inches (after Dixon).

Coiled type Atsugewi hopper basket with flying geese design. View shows pounding hole in bottom of basket, in this case bound with buckskin.

of Maidu patterns exhibit a more or less obscure realism which
becomes apparent only after one is informed as to what the design
means.   The Maidu show a tendency also toward arrangement of
design elements in spiral or zigzag lines.

Dixon noted that "mussel's tongue" (the fresh water mussel)
is one of the unique and peculiar basketry designs used by the
Atsugewi. Representation of intestines and deer excrement are also
worthy of special mention for this tribe.   Other common Atsugewi
designs in basketry decoration are lizard, deer rib, owl's claw, and
flying geese, as well as arrow-point. Two or more different designs
are often combined on a single basket.   Among Atsugewi and
Achomawi there seems to be no restriction of certain patterns to
baskets intended for special uses.   Like mountain Maidu, zigzag
and spiral arrangements are preferred, horizontal bands being rare.
Curiously an Atsugewi design is often given different meaning by
different individual Indians.   This is in contrast to the uniformity
of interpretation of a given design by all the Maidu individuals,
normally.

Yana tribes frequently substituted another material for willow
ribs.   The identity of this warp is not certain. Reliable students
believe it to be hazelnut twigs, but to my knowledge that plant is
scarce indeed even in the foothill territory.   Yana and Yahi had
some other peculiarities in their basketry.   Designs were sometimes wrought in a negative way, that is by merely leaving off
overlay so that the design was thereby defined in exposed pine
root weft.   Sapir and Spier found that these tribes also used alder
bark for dying basketry decoration materials a red-brown. A reddish
color was produced on peeled shield fern stems by passing them
through the mouth while chewing dogwood bark.   They dyed pine

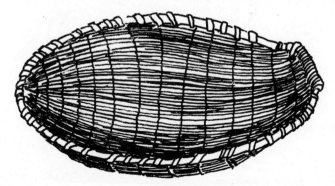

Maidu open twined "tray" or plate-like basket about ten inches long
(after Dixon)

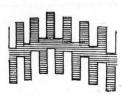

Maidu fish - teeth design on coiled basket.

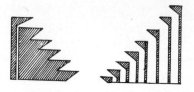

Mountain Maidu mountains designs on twined baskets. The right hand treatment may be repeated in reverse to the right making a symmetrical pyramid shaped design outline.

Mountain Maidu geese-flying design on coiled basket.

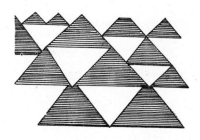

An interesting unsymmetrical flower design.

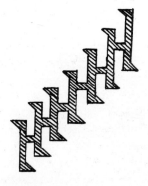

Atsugewi lizard's claw or lizard's foot design.

Atsugewi intestines.

roots, too, on occasion with a red soil or with the powdery filling of spores from the inside of a fungus obtained from certain coniferous trees. These variations of basketry decoration do not seem to have been used by the Atsugewi and mountain Maidu.

The basketry described above was all close-woven. In fact, so closely were the twined baskets made that they held water with little or no leakage even without linings of pitch or any other substance. There was no pottery of any kind in central or northern California.

The art of basketry included also a third type---loose or open weaving, sometimes of tules. The latter were also used extensively for making mats for a variety of purposes. Open weaving at other times was done with willow withes, split juniper twigs, or of another material tentatively identified as hazel. Fish traps, carrying baskets, some storage baskets, and bags were not infrequently of this type of construction.

All basketry materials had to be well soaked in water, as they were brittle when dry. After weaving and upon drying these materials set in place, making the basketry firm, strong, and resistant to unraveling.

Collection of basketry materials was more arduous and required greater know-how than might be suspected. Willow withes were only taken from the particularly strong and supple shoots from Hinds or valley willow *(Salix hindsiana)* which grows along stream banks up to 3000 foot elevations and also from the similar sandbar, river, or grey willow *(Salix fluviatilis* variety *argyrophylla)* which also lines streams, often growing in sandbars. These species are recognized by their long very narrow silvery leaves and a grey bark, furrowed when mature. Willow twigs were collected when the leaves were off of the stems in the spring and in the fall. At other times the twigs were more brittle. Spring picked willow withes "slipped" their bark easily, but those collected in the fall had to be scraped to remove the bark. The willow ribs were further dressed by scraping to uniform size.

Pine roots of either ponderosa pine *(Pinus ponderosa)* or digger pine *(Pinus sabiniana)* were usually used. However not all trees had roots of suitable strength and flexibility, so that it was necessary to "shop around" for good roots. This involved digging holes to reach the roots and then testing these by tugging on small strands until suitable roots were located. Roots three or four inches in diameter were then cut off with a small obsidian axe, if the individual were so fortunate as to possess this rarity, or by using a sort

Atsugewi twined basket, deer-
rib and arrow point designs.
Both are frequently used.

Atsugewi deer-gut design on
twined basket — also a popular
pattern.

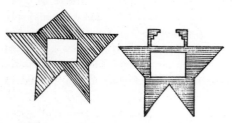

Pit River (used by Dixon to include
Atsugewi) popular mussels' tongue
designs.

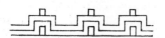

Another Atsugewi version of
deer-gut design on twined
basket.

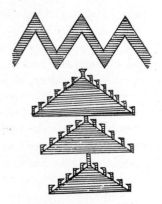

Mountain Maidu mountain —
and — cloud design on
coiled basket.

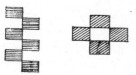

Pit River (applied by Dixon to
include also the Atsugewi) deer
excrement designs.

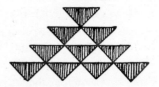

Atsugewi pine cone design

Atsugewi flint design

of bone pick, or, more commonly, by slowly burning through the green root with a small fire. Root lengths of about four feet were gathered, taken home, and there roasted in hot ashes. This made the pine roots very soft. They were then split into quarters with digging sticks or stone choppers and finally were pulled apart into thin strips using hands and teeth. The resulting half inch wide strips were tied into bundles for storage. In use, these strips were well soaked in water. Pine root strands of proper width were easily split off by hand. The finer and smaller the basketry to be done, naturally, the narrower was the material split for making it.

The chief overlay material --- already mentioned --- was what we call bear-grass or squaw-grass. In truth this is not grass, but the leaf of a lily, the well known bear-grass of Mount Rainier National Park, scientifically known as *Xerophylum tenax.* This grows only in limited areas in this region, hence Atsugewi had to make long trips on foot to obtain it. In recent years, at least, bear-grass was to be found only in the territory of the Shasta and of the mountain Maidu: a few miles west of Mount Shasta and near Green-ville in Plumas County. Bear-grass could be collected only during about two weeks in mid-July. Earlier it was too tender; later it was too brittle "like hay". Only new central leaves of each plant were plucked. The heavy mid-rib had to be removed from each leaf with an awl before use.

Maidenhair fern frond stems were picked in August.

Redbud twigs collected in the spring would "slip" the red outer bark easily in a thin layer. This was used for overlay pattern making on twined baskets. The white inner bark, or, more properly, sapwood was then stripped off for binding material and as the white lashing weft for coiled baskets. In the case of fall-collected red-bud twigs the red outer bark adhered to the sapwood. This was used as the lashing strand or weft where red designs were desired on coiled baskets.

Apwaruge, the eastern division of the Atsugewi, often made baskets of tules. These were more flexible, softer baskets than those made by the westerners, the Atsuge, and so there was con-siderable exchange of baskets between the two divisions of the Atsugewi.

Atsugewi occasionally made openwork baskets from split juniper too, especially for low scoop-shaped, round, or oval baskets for fishing, root cleaning, et cetera, but as indicated earlier, willow ribs were used for this purpose also.

Basket styles varied little among the several tribes of the

(Yana) dogs ears

Probably Yana house design

Maidu quail tip design widely
used but only on coiled baskets.

(Yana) crane's leg (Atsugewi) meadow lark
neck

(Achomawi) flying geese or
pine cone
(Yana) pine cone

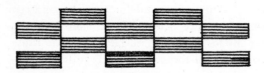

Maidu earthworm design on a coiled basket.

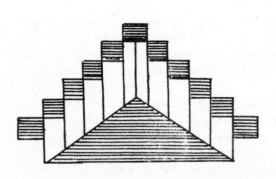

Maidu bushes design on a coiled basket.

Mountain Maidu
duck's-wing design
on a coiled basketry
plaque.

(Maidu) diamond
(Yana) wolf's eye

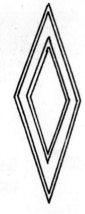

(Atsugewi) flint or
arrowhead

Mountain Maidu
eye design.

(Maidu) watersnake (?)
(Yana) bushes

(Yana) bats

Maidu design,
probably sugar
pine tree.

A continuing zig-zig arrow feather design
widely and frequently used by Maidu in coiled
basketry, sometimes this was combined with
the quail tip pattern.

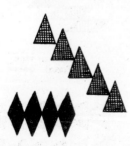

Single and double arrow point designs — the most commonly used of all
Maidu patterns. It was relatively easy to make and very versatile.

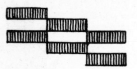

(Maidu) big tongues
(Yana)   intestines

(Maidu) quail tip
(Yana)   root digger

(Maidu) mountain
(Yana)   root digger hand

(Maidu) earthworm
(Yana)   intestines

(Maidu) earthworm
(Yana)   intestines

(Maidu) mountain
(Yana)   root digger hand

(Achomawi) mountain or
           bear's foot
(Yana)   root digger hand

(Maidu) vine
(Yana) geese

(Maidu) rattlesnake
(Yana) geese

(Wintun) sucker tail
(Yana)   long worms in
          rotten wood.

(Yana) wolf's eye

Lassen r e g i o n. Bottle shapes were never made until after the coming of white man. Cooking baskets were bowl-shaped with high, convexly curved sides, sometimes nearly globular in form. Baskets from which food was eaten individually and general utility baskets were similarly shaped but smaller. Boiling baskets were sometimes without decoration; their dimensions of height and width were about equal. Storage baskets also had about the same shape, curving less, sometimes, but were large, being three feet or more in size. Some were of open work, but usually they were of close or tight weaving.

Flatish bowls or somewhat c u r v e d trays were used for food platters as well as for winnowing, parching, and cleaning foods by chafing. Some were of open weave made of willow or hazel (?) only while others were closely woven.

Basketry acorn grinding hoppers also called milling baskets or pounding baskets, were usually regular twined baskets of suitable size and shape: wide mouthed bowl or funnel-shaped. Having no central point from which to start the warp, because of the open bottoms, hopper baskets were started by twining three pine root wefts about the bases of many willow warps to make a circle about five inches in diameter. Additional warps were built up on the radiating ribs, proceeding then in the normal manner of twining. Twined hopper baskets were usually reinforced by lashing one or two strong rings of willow or serviceberry withes. They might also be bound with b u c k s k i n along the b o t t o m edges for improved strength and durability as well as to decrease loss of acorn meal during the pounding process. In recent years both mountain Maidu and Atsugewi, also used coiling t e c h n i q u e in making hopper baskets, for which purpose it is well suited.

A recent innovation among Atsugewi has been the covering of bottles with basketry and also the weaving of oblong shaped closely twined and coiled baskets, as well as goblet shaped creations.

According to Garth, the seed beater ". . . . was a paddle-shaped implement from one and a half to two feet long with a willow warp and open work twining, also of willow (spaced at three quarters of an inch between rows) across the blade. The handle was w r a p p e d either with w i l l o w strips or with buckskin."

Another important use of basketry was in the construction of cradle boards, or more properly, basket cradles. These are generally known to present day Americans by the incorrect term papoose baskets. The cradle basket is discussed under the heading "Birth

(Yurok) flint
(Yana) zigzagging

(Maidu) quail-tip
(Yana) "sitting up
      in a series"

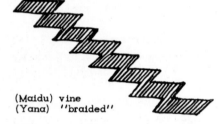

(Maidu) vine
(Yana) "braided"

(Yana) mussels

(Yana) mountains

(Yurok) "sitting"
(Yana) "ziggagging
      and turning back"

(Maidu) earthworm
(Yana) "braided"

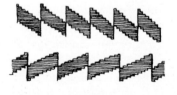

(Yana) flint

(Yana) wolf's eye

(Yana) trout or
salmon tails

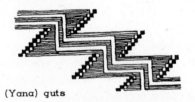

(Yana) guts

(Atsugewi) skunk's ear

and Babies''.

Beautifully made basketry caps for women, finely twined, spreading bowl-shaped affairs were made by all tribes of the Lassen area.   These were nicely decorated on the bottoms---or rather tops---as well as on the sides, a feature lacking on all other types of local baskets.   Another unique feature of the basketry cap was the fact that the inside of the hat was abraded by rubbing so that none of the pattern remained visible because all of the overlay on the inside had been worn away.   It is suspected that this made the inside of the hat less slippery on the hair so that it did not slip off the head so easily.   Removal of the decoration from the inside of the basketry cap in no way altered the appearance or permanence of the outside decorative patterns.

Mats were woven of viscid bulrush, more commonly called tule stalks *(Scirpus lacustris* or *acutus)*.   According to Voegelin, Atsugewi sometimes sewed these together by piercing them with bone needles.   However the more usual method of manufacture was that of lashing together the ends of parallel tule stalks laid next to each other.   This was done with double cords or strands in the regular simple twining manner which shows up well in the sketch of Atsugewi tule leggings.   Such mats were extensively used as bed mats or mattresses, as earth wall coverings, as doorway and ventilator hole hangings, and so on by all of the tribes of the Lassen region.   Mountain Maidu also employed broad-leaved cat-tail *(Typha latifolia)* or narrow-leaved cat-tail *(Typha angustifolia)* for such purposes on occasion.   This tribe also appears to have used a string weft in making at least some of the mats.

Chapter XII
TANNING, CORDAGE, AND GLUE

Mountain Maidu buried bear skins in wet ground, but hides generally were soaked about a week in water by local Indians. Mountain Maidu used ashes to help dehair skins other than deer, but this was not a practice common to other tribes. Stone, or more frequently, shaped deer rib or pelvic bones were used as dehairing scraper tools on skins. The hide was draped over an inclined post and was soaked and squeezed occasionally during the process of scraping.

The tanning agent was a cooked soup of animal brains, particularly those of deer. This material might first have been mashed, mixed with dry moss, and then molded into small cakes for drying and storage. The deer brain agent was well rubbed into the cleaned, soaked skin. It was then allowed to soak overnight in the tanning solution. The next day while drying the skin in the sun, the operator stretched and worked the hide with his hands to make it soft and pliable.

Among Atsugewi the skin was then smoked over a fire of moist rotten logs or green juniper boughs burning in a shallow pit. The skin was laid on a domed framework of willow branches arched over the fire. The hide was turned occasionally to insure uniform treatment. Mr. Garth believes that this smoking process was recently learned. It was not generally practiced by neighboring tribes, but produced superior buckskin which resisted stiffening as a result of subsequent wetting. Even Atsugewi did not smoke other skins.

Men did all this work as well as the hunting, skinning, and fashioning of garments from hides. Skins were sewn with bone awls and deer sinew thread which was made by rolling fine deer

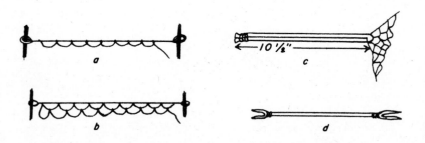

Nets. a, b, stages in net making; c, tule float; d, net shuttle.

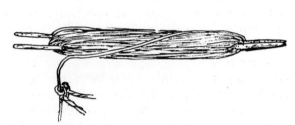

Net making shuttle about fourteen
inches long (after Dixon)

The usual Maidu knot
for nets (after Dixon)

Carrying net

sinew strands on the thigh with the open hand.

Like other local tribes, the Maidu used many woven skin
blankets.. These were fashioned from one inch strips of rabbit fur,
especially, but also of the skins of wildcat, cougar, geese, or crows.
These were not tanned so that upon drying they twisted or curled
like the strands of a rope with the fur or feather side out. Ends
were tied together to form a long fur or feather covered rope. This
was wound about two poles set upright in the ground six feet or so
apart to form the warp for the blanket. More of the same material
was then woven up and down as weft to produce a soft and very
warm skin blanket which was also quite durable. When bird skins
were employed a cord core was threaded thru the center of the
twisted strands before weaving for greater strength.

Mountain Maidu also did feather work like that of the Atsugewi,
however foothill and valley Maidu did so to a greater extent and
of a more elaborate nature.

Willow, serviceberry, and redbud withes, and at lower elevations, lengths of wild grape vines were used for tying purposes.
However, Indians also had need for strong and more versatile and
more durable string, cord, and rope. These were usually made from
vegetable fibers. Atsugewi and mountain Maidu used Indian hemp
and milkweed but not nettle or iris fibers as did some other tribes.
When mature, but before they became old and brittle, the plants
were collected and dried, stripped of leaves, and the flesh was
scraped and pounded off leaving the free fibers. String was made
by placing two small bundles of fibers parallel and close together
on the thigh of the leg. These were rolled up into two strands side
by side with one stroke of the open hand moving either up or down
the thigh. On the return stroke the two separate and now twisted
strands were twisted together into one string. Stout cord was made
by repeating the process, substituting two strings for the two
bundles of loose fibers this time. To make rope the process
was repeated several times, successively doubling the cordage
product. As the cordage strands were twined together, the product
was held in the left hand, the rolling being done by the right hand
on the right thigh.

Nets of good quality were fabricated in a variety of mesh sizes,
the uniformity of which was controlled by use of squarish wooden
blocks. Shuttles to hold the string for net tying were straight pieces
of wood notched at each end and into which the strand was wrapped.
As has been pointed out, nets were used chiefly for hunting, fishing, and carrying, although small nets were often worn in the hair
by men.

Adhesives were important in the economy of the Indians too.
Pine pitch and glue made from the skins of fish were used. A
solution of the latter was mixed by the mountain Maidu with certain
internal organs of fish and boiled vegetable materials to improve
the quality of their glue.

Chapter XIII
TRANSPORTATION

It was the lack of transportation rather than the existence of any which was important to the aboriginal Americans. This was responsible for the degree of isolation which was required to produce the variety of customs and languages in most parts of the "New World". Introduction of the horse in historic times materially changed the habits of Plains Indians. Likewise the somewhat aggressive Modoc tribe to the north of the Pit River, whose conflict with the whites has been memorialized in Lava Beds National Monument today, became mobile, even prior to the gold rush days, through use of the horse. As a result the Modocs made a number of hit and run raids upon Atsugewi and other tribes and were able to carry off slaves. This was not the traditional mode of warfare.

Transportation among Indians was by foot or by water until recent times. California Indians did not use dogs as beasts of burden as Plains Indians did and as the Eskimos still do. Women did general hauling; men, however, did most of the really heavy carrying. Women used the conical burden basket extensively, but the men did not. Both sexes used the buckskin pack strap which in the case of mountain Maidu passed over the top of the head. Atsugewi pack straps went over the forehead and also over the shoulder across the chest. The brimless basketry cap or hat was used with the packstrap especially among the women. Heavy loads were frequently carried by men upon the shoulder; such burdens were often rolled in mats or animal skins.

Carrying nets made of twisted fibers were commonly employed by men and women among local tribes. Atsugewi used a folded buckskin bag sewed at the edges, with a handle on top, and opening at the side. Yana manufactured an open-work carrying basket too.

In this region loads were never carried on the head, but on occasion might be suspended on a pole and carried between two men. The mountain Maidu also used a litter for the sick, but Atsugewi carried sick persons in burden baskets on their backs.

In rough country crude trails were sometimes built, but this was not a common practice. Generally trails as such were not constructed, but where they existed they had developed as the result of long use along logical routes, in much the same manner as deer and other game trails develop.

To cross streams advantage was taken of logs which had fallen of natural causes. On occasion single logs were felled by burning

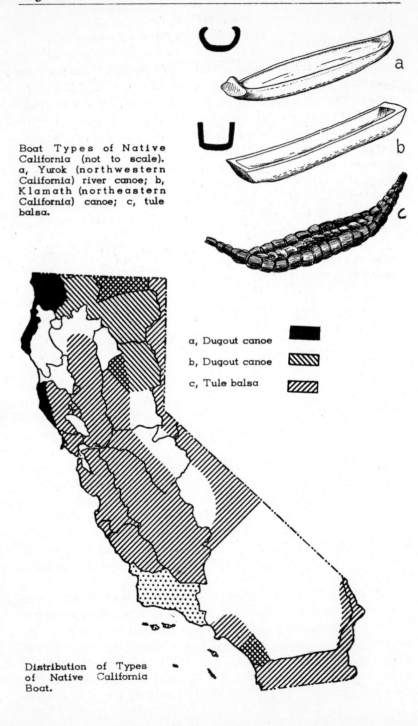

Boat Types of Native California (not to scale). a, Yurok (northwestern California) river canoe; b, Klamath (northeastern California) canoe; c, tule balsa.

a, Dugout canoe

b, Dugout canoe

c, Tule balsa

Distribution of Types of Native California Boat.

Atsugewi dug-out canoe on Hat Creek

to serve as bridges. Yana at lower elevations frequently had large streams to cross and smaller trees to utilize. Two logs might be felled parallel and cross sticks lashed on with grapevine for better footing.

In swimming most Indians used a pseudo-breast stroke or swam on their backs with a frog style stroke. Atsugewi also did a "dog paddle" keeping arms under water. Mountain Maidu used swimming techniques which embraced principles like those of white man's side stroke and crawl. They jumped into the water feet first in preference to headfirst diving. When swimming under water to collect crawfish or mussels a rock was often tied loosely to the back.

Water transportation was not of the same degree of importance to the tribes of the Lassen region that it was to Sacramento Valley, Coastal, and Northwestern Indians. Nevertheless Atsugewi used sharp or blunt ended canoes while that of the mountain Maidu had a shovel-like prow and stern. These were made from pine logs, usually windfalls about two feet in diameter and had a capacity of two to four persons. The logs were hollowed out by controlled burning so that the walls were an inch or two thick. Pitch was rubbed onto portions needing more burning. Water or mud were used to check burning and the charred wood was scraped out with rough angular stones. Local dugout canoes were rather crude affairs. Cracking of the wood was prevented by keeping the boats wet. They were propelled by an unadorned poling rod or by a single bladed square-ended paddle about three feet long. A raft, consisting of three or four logs lashed together, was used as well by all local tribes and propelled by poling.

Atsugewi had another type of craft: the tule balsa---a five foot long raised prow affair made of bundles of tules lashed together. It might be poled or else pushed by a swimmer. Often this raft-like boat was towed by a rope of willow. Atsugewi occasionally ferried children or goods in baskets, while among mountain Maidu swimmers carried children on their backs and carried goods in one hand, raised above the water level, swimming with the other hand.

Chapter XIV
DOMESTICATED ANIMALS AND PETS

We are apt to think of Indians, especially Plains Indians, riding horses as part of the natural prehistoric scene, yet this was not the case. Although fossil remains in the rocks show clearly the development of the horse over a period of several millions of years on this continent, the horse, the camel, and the rhinoceros ---to mention but a few of the spectacular mammals---became extinct on the American continents before the advent of prehistoric man. American Indians had never seen a horse until the coming of the Spanish to the New World in 1540. Likewise domestic cattle, sheep, goats, and chickens were unknown to the aborigines.

The dog was widely distributed, however. Some tribes had large as well as small dogs of a variety of colors. In the Lassen area the dogs were all about the size of small coyotes, mostly with fairly short hair, but there are some reports of long haired dogs. Typically the dogs had small rather erect and pointed ears. Coloration was chiefly fawn colored to brown. Amongst Atsugewi, dogs were usually quite numerous, but certain villages seem to have had only a few. In such cases and among the mountain Maidu, who generally had only few dogs, they were borrowed for hunting. Dogs were almost always named.

Dogs served to warn their owners of the approach of strangers to the village or camp. Mountain Maidu taught their dogs not to bark, but to "snif" conspicuously as a signal of stranger approach.

Tribes of the Lassen area did not normally keep dogs in their dwelling houses. Atsugewi built separate, domed, bark-covered dog houses, and mountain Maidu built two kinds of shelters for their dogs. One was a subterranean earth-covered dog house, and the other a conical affair of bark slab type construction.

Dogs were widely used in hunting. They were efficient in catching rodents and other small mammals such as ground hogs. They were also useful for treeing mountain lions and were adept at bringing down wounded deer by jumping up and seizing the deers' ears.

Dogs were not often eaten by tribes in this section of California. Upon death, dogs were not buried, but the bodies were merely thrown out.

Upon death of the dog's owner, among Atsugewi, the dog was retained by the widow, but among mountain Maidu the dog was suspended in a tree because "It makes dog's spirit glad"! Although not being generally considered in this account, it is curious that among Modoc and eastern Achomawi dogs were burned at the deaths of their owners.

Bear cubs were commonly kept. Atsugewi also kept fawns and other small mammals as pets. Birds of various sorts were kept by certain tribes. Atsugewi plucked or cut wings of birds, especially of eagles whose feathers were prized for arrow making, and for ceremonial and decorative purposes.

Chapter XV
CLOTHING

The members of all tribes, especially the Yana and Yahi, went bareheaded much of the time. However, b a s k e t r y caps nearly hemispherical in shape and of fine tightly twined weave were worn regularly by Indian women. The caps were probably worn to prevent chafing of the pack straps originally, but Atsugewi women wore them most of the time. Such hats were well decorated with overlaid designs typical of the tribes under consideration. Those of Yana and Yahi were u s u a l l y of tule with black and white o v e r l a y. Mountain Maidu made some coiled basketry caps, not infrequently employing tules or reeds.

Men of all our tribes wore fur headbands on occasion and among Atsugewi, fur or buckskin caps too, especially in winter, when shallow bucket shaped skin hats of coyote, raccoon, mink and the like afforded protection against the rather intense cold.

Eyeshades attached to a band around the head were worn by some Yana women so as not to see their sons-in-law! Atsugewi men and possibly others might wear side blinds when spearing fish at night to keep torch light out of their eyes.

Children up to about six years of age ran about naked, and often the older men and w o m e n did likewise, particularly among the Maidu.

Buckskin dresses were worn to some extent by the women of most local t r i b e s. The mountain Maidu dress was tied at both s houlders and tied or belted at the waist. The garment was provided with flaps over the upper arms but lacked sleeves. Buckskin dresses were worn by some Indian women rich in worldly goods, and usually for special occasions. Recent buckskin dresses, of course, are sewn on sewing machines, neatly tailored, and follow the general pattern of the conventional dress, including regular sleeves.

In normal everyday garb Indian women were naked above the waist. A wrap-around skirt, or, more frequently two narrow or wide aprons were worn. Sometimes one apron went around the hips, being tied in back and provided with a buckskin flap which covered the wearer's buttocks. The Indian women's aprons were commonly made of shredded incense-cedar, willow, or juniper bark, or of tules. In the case of Yana and Yahi women, frequently grass or shredded, spring-gathered, broad-leaf maple bark were used. The latter was a favorite valley Maidu skirt material. The double aprons might

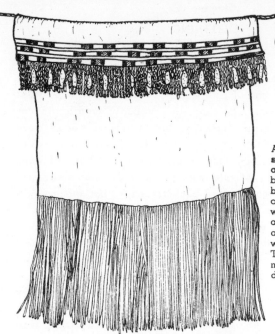

A beautiful old Shasta buckskin woman's wrap-around
apron ornamented with tan,
black, and red vegetable fiber
bound slitting in the manner
of coarse modern hemstitching,
with strings of olivella shells
and shaped abolone pendants,
and finished on the bottom
with long buckskin fringes.
The garment is much like the
more pretentious aprons
described for Atsugewi

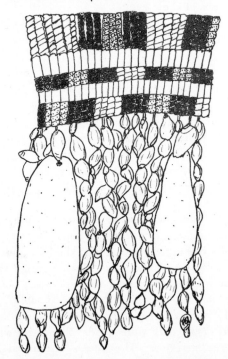

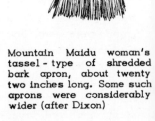

Mountain Maidu woman's
tassel-type of shredded
bark apron, about twenty
two inches long. Some such
aprons were considerably
wider (after Dixon)

Detail of ornamentation on the Shasta buckskin apron

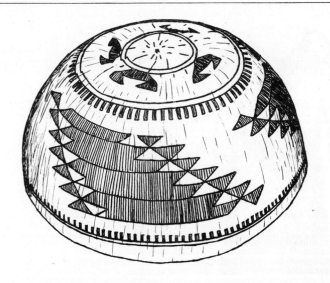

Woman's basketry cap probably Atsugewi or Shasta.   Note the design placed on top as well as on the sides of the basket, in contrast to other types of baskets.   The bottoms of which are devoid both of design and overlay materials and so present an unadorned pine-root surface.

however be made of whole buckskin or of strips or cords of buckskin, and in winter furs might be used for the purpose. The double apron is recognized as the standard garb of California Indian women. That of the Maidu was often very narrow, being not much more than a front and a rear tassel.

Women's casual aprons and other clothing were not highly ornamented, but "dress-up" clothes might be fairly elaborately trimmed. Fringing of buckskin, spangles of shell money and ornaments, strings of shell beads, pine nuts, deer hoofs, and special white grass fringes commonly decorated their better clothes.

In the summer some men, and particularly old ones wore nothing at all. Most others wore very little clothing besides a sort of loin covering of buckskin or fur which went between the legs and was held in place back and front by a belt about the waist. A crude buckskin shirt without sleeves was sometimes used.

During winter above aprons, skirts, or loin covering other garments were worn. Then men commonly wore the sleeveless buckskin shirt. Both sexes usually wore robes of woven rabbit skins (usually imported by the Atsugewi), or made of deer or bear fur and worn with the hair side inside. Or else the robes were of a patchwork

Atsugewi fringed buckskin dress of
pioneer period

of small mammal skins sewn together. These same robes were
frequently used for bedding at night. As a matter of fact almost
any sort of skins available might be used as robes. These were
tied on in a variety of ways. The wearers must have presented a
rather motley appearance. On occasion small poncho style robes
with a central hole for the head and neck clothed the upper bodies
of local Indians during cold weather.

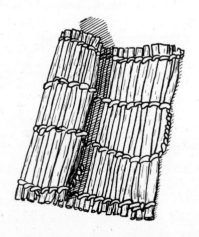

An Atsugewi legging made of lashing
tules together with a simple twining
stitch

Maidu buckskin moccasin
about eleven inches long
(after Dixon)

Thumbless mittens were made of cased skins of weasels, rats or small cottontail rabbits and tied at the wrist with a thong. Atsugewi also utilized their fur-lined quivers as muffs when hunting.

California Indians spent much of the time barefoot, but wore buckskin moccasins at war, on long hunts or journeys. Different styles were made by each of the local tribes. None, however, were normally decorated. Mountain Maidu also made moccasins of fur with the hair side in, and Atsugewi stuffed pounded grass or grass into their footwear or wore grass or tule slippers inside their moccasins during the winter. Maidu put soft grass or sedges in their moccasins for added warmth. An extra sole of tougher leather such as elkskin was sometimes sewn onto the moccasin, but this was not customary.

Occasionally open sandals held on by three or four thongs were worn by Atsugewi and Yana.

Knee length leggings of various materials were common in winter. These were tied on with buckskin strips at ankle and knee. Yana used hip-length pantleg type leggings held on with waist

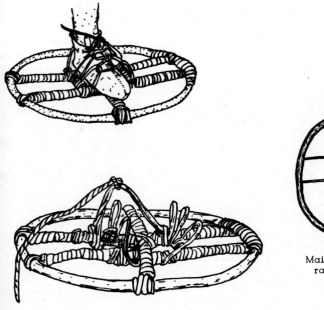

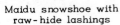

toe strap

Maidu snowshoe with
raw-hide lashings

Snowshoe of about eighteen inches in
diameter (after Dixon)

bands. Atsugewi sometimes employed fur pieces, twined tule, or spiral wrap-around fur strip leggings. Maidu used deerhide leggings with the hair side inside. These went from ankles to above the knees where they were tied, and were held close to the leg by an outside spirally wound thong from top to bottom.

Snowshoes were a necessity too in the rigorous climate of even the lower portions of the areas inhabited by tribes of the Lassen area, particularly in those of the Atsugewi and mountain Maidu. Snowshoes of the former Indians were circular in plan; those of the latter were oval. Snowshoes were fashioned from small green wooden limbs shaped while hot, and then crisscrossed with strips of buckskin or hide with the fur side down for better traction. Atsugewi used green juniper limbs for the purpose. Since the whole foot was bound firmly to this footgear, there was no heel play as in the case of white mans' snowshoes.

Chapter XVI
BEAUTY AND PERSONAL GROOMING

Of Atsugewi standards of beauty Garth states: "The ideal woman was short but plump and solidly built so that she could do much work. A slim woman was considered too weak, and a very tall woman was made fun of and called lohkata (stick woman). Heavy breasts, a straight slim nose, large eyes, long black hair, and small feet were all admirable qualities. A girl with big feet was likely to be lazy, also a small foot was desirable because it would not take so large a moccasin. A mother pressed her girl child's foot together to make it slender. The ideal man was of average height and was heavy set. If a child had a flat nose, his mother pinched it and tried to give it a higher bridge. Bow legs, it was said, might be straightened by the mother when the child was young. Also a child's ears were pressed against his head; if the ears stood out, this was thought to indicate poor hearing. A slim hand indicated a lazy person; a short stubby hand signified a good worker."

Garth also comments to the effect that evidently the ideals of Indian beauty had a very practical basis. The same general criteria of beauty and desirability of women seem to have prevailed among the other tribes of this region also, but Yana preferred a rather flat and broad faced feminine beauty.

The hair of both men and women among California Indians was generally worn long. The tribes of the Lassen area were no exception. However, bangs on the forehead were known. Boys and girls let their hair hang loosely, except that Atsugewi sometimes cut small boy's hair short to make it grow better later.

Women usually parted their hair in the middle wearing it in two hanks, one hanging in front of each shoulder. Each was tied with a piece of rawhide. Women of Yana tribes often used strips of otter or mink fur for the purpose as did some Atsugewi. Yana women might add further decoration in the form of a small string of shell beads. Atsugewi women might paint their scalps at the part in the hair with red paint.

The male Indian tied his hair in a bunch which hung down the back. All local tribes, except mountain Maidu, seem also to have frequently used a small mesh hairnet made of plant fibers with a buckskin band to hold a man's hair in a sort of roll at the back of his head. Maidu called the net wee-kah. In preparation for war or

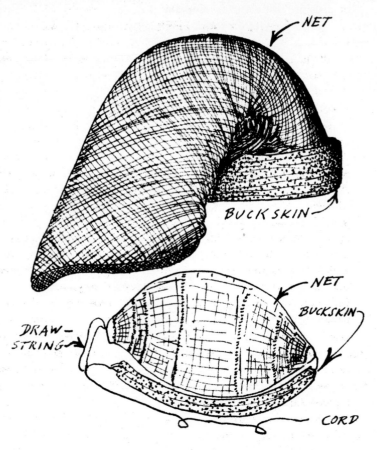

Men's hair net type of cap worn by adult males of all Lassen area tribes, the wearer's long hair being piled on top of the head when worn as in upper sketch (after Dixon) with the loose excess net allowed to fall straight down behind.

for the hunt Yana men coiled their hair on their heads with well defined top knots. For dances and other special events, male Maidu and Yana, if rich, wore mesh bonnets thickly covered with white eagle down feathers tied in so that the net strands were not visible. Bone hairpins were sometimes used among Yana and mountain Maidu men.

Adults cut their hair off with stone knives to show grief and mourning when relatives died. Both men and women cropped their hair closely, but mountain Maidu women sometimes only trimmed it off to shoulder length. Singeing instead of cutting the hair was sometimes resorted to.

For combing the hair, Atsugewi might use a single stick, a pine cone, or a teasle burr. Mountain Maidu might use stiff pine needles, but the item most commonly used by all tribes for the purpose was the porcupine tail. The animal's tail was skinned out, stuffed with grass, and sewed shut at the open end. Sharp ends of the porcupine quills were blunted with hot stones.

Hair was not dyed in this region. It was, however, rubbed with animal fat or bone marrow to make it look nicer by aboriginal standards. Atsugewi are said to have perfumed their hair on occasion with aromatic plant foliage. Hair and body lice were not uncommon; these were hunted and removed by hand. Maidu washed their hair frequently with common soaproot *(Chlorogalum pomeridianmum).*

Faces of adults were painted for a number of occasions. Black was used to some extent by both sexes to prevent sunburn and snow-blindness if long exposure in the bright sun were expected. Although Yana men and women used red and white paint when dancing, among our other tribes face paint was used chiefly by men for dances and ceremonies.

Paint pigments were mixed with animal fat, especially deer grease, or with marrow and applied with the fingers. It was smeared on upper arms, legs, chest, and cheeks. Atsugewi and mountain Maidu blackened their eyebrows. Red pigment was either red soil, usually roasted or burned to make the color brighter, or the spores from a fungus which grows on the bark of fir trees. The fungus

Porcupine tail comb about ten inches long (after Dixon)

material was dried over a slow fire to prepare it for use. Black pigment was universally charcoal. Ashes were not used as white pigment. Students of local tribes state that chalk was employed for white paint. However, chalk is lacking in the Lassen vicinity and it is highly probable that the suitable and readily available white diatomaceous earth deposits were used for this purpose instead. Atsugewi also used blue color which was obtained in rock form by trade with their northern Pit River or Achomawi neighbors.

The light beards which started to grow on male Indians' faces were universally removed completely by plucking with the fingers.

Earlobe and nose piercing was generally practiced by both sexes. Among Atsugewi rims of their ears as well as the lobes were perforated in some instances.

Tattooing was occasionally done by Yana, but not as commonly as among Atsugewi where women not infrequently wore tattooed vertical lines across their mouths. Both sexes commonly tattooed their cheeks with horizontal lines or with two or three lines radiating from the corners of the mouth. Arms and legs were also tattooed to a certain extent. The mutilation was done by rubbing charcoal into cuts which had been made with stone knives or by rubbing charcoal on the skin and then pricking it with bone awls or porcupine quills. However, even among Atsugewi, tattooing was by no means universal. Mountain Maidu women were sometimes tattooed with three, five, or seven vertical lines on the chin.

Earings were worn by nearly all men and women. Atsugewi employed bone rings, clamshell beads, feathers and even painted ear ornaments. Mountain Maidu and Yana usually used bone or wooden ones, plain or decorated with feathers or shells. Abalone, like other sea shells, were received only in trade and were fashioned into pendants for ears or noses.

Nose piercing consisted of making a hole through the septum of the nose. This practice was popular among all local tribes. It was done to permit the wearing of jewelry although Yana ascribed a deeper meaning to the custom as well. They believed that no person would go to his equivalent of heaven unless the nose septum was pierced. Hence this was done to the dead and a stick inserted if it had not been done in life. Two-pointed bone nose-pins were popular inserts as were long narrow dentalium shells, or nose pendants of beads. Only among mountain Maidu were nose ornaments highly decorated.

Necklaces were common adornments too, but local tribes did

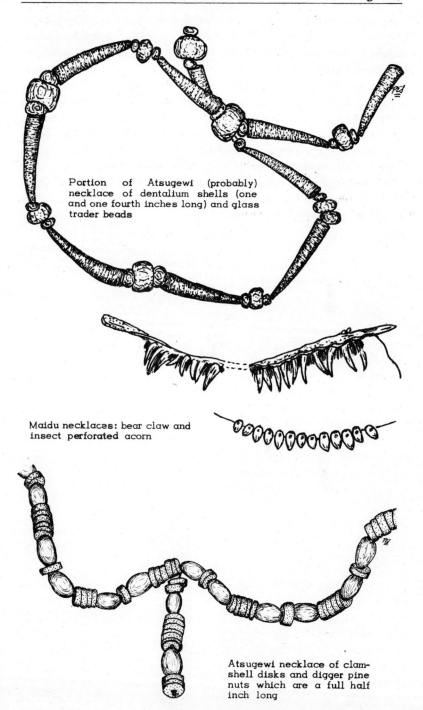

Portion of Atsugewi (probably) necklace of dentalium shells (one and one fourth inches long) and glass trader beads

Maidu necklaces: bear claw and insect perforated acorn

Atsugewi necklace of clamshell disks and digger pine nuts which are a full half inch long

not use bracelets. Items used for necklaces were perhaps bear teeth and bear claws among Atsugewi and Yana. More commonly, certainly, and used by all of our tribes were olivella shells, shaped pieces of abalone shells, small animal and bird bone rings or tubes, clamshell discs, long tooth-shells (dentalia), and Digger Pine nuts which had been parched until blackened. Their ends had then been rubbed off or holes bored through ends or sides and cleaned out. Yana also made mussel shell disks locally, not only for necklaces but as ear pendants. In later years all tribes used glass trader beads, usually interspersed with native items.

Maidu, especially their tribes of the lower elevations, went in for elaborate feather decorations and headresses. Valley Maidu even had feather cloaks for ceremonial use.

Chapter XVII
WEALTH

Among local tribes wealth was the direct result of skill and industry and was highly regarded by all. A person's social status in the tribe varied directly with his wealth. Lazy persons not able to properly care for their own needs were considered as bums and looked down upon by all other members of the village. With wealth went a certain amount of power. Chiefs, although empowered by heritage, were always well to do, and the wealthiest men in smaller units acted in the capacity of head-men.

As with modern man, money among Indians was an arbitrary medium of exchange, yet it was of more practical value to the Indians than our own coins are to us. Their money was prized not only for what it would buy in material things, but as possessing important decorative value as well.

The long tooth-shell or dentalium was used whole and unmodified. It was the currency of the northwest California coast. The money of central and southern California was the clamshell disk. This was cut, smoothed into disk shapes about half an inch in diameter, and each was perforated with a central hole by means of which this money could be strung onto cords. In no case did local tribes travel the California coast to obtain these shell coins. Instead, this item found its way to Indians of the interior through progressive or step-by-step trading from coastal tribes through intermediate aboriginal traders.

As we might expect, dentalia, having a northern origin, were secured by Atsugewi not from their neighbors to the south, but from the northern Yana in exchange for buckskins, arrows, wildcat skin quivers, and woodpecker scalps. The mountain Maidu did not have dentalia at all.

Except for the central Yana custom of measuring the length of strings of clamshell disks, amounts of money were determined by counting and not by measuring length on arm tatoos as was so commonly the case in other parts of California. Skins of small mammals which had been skinned by making only one slit in the hind quarters and whose mouth openings had been tied shut, served as purses.

All of our tribes used clamshell money. Among Yana clamshell disks were not as valuable as dentalia, and they were more common also among Atsugewi, the dentalia being used more for decoration than as money. The tribes of the Lassen region generally received the finished clamshell money; almost never did they manufacture this, although they did work traded abalone shell into jewelry pieces.

Material wealth or treasure other than weapons, skins, baskets, and food also consisted largely of imported seashells. Whole olivella shells were commonly used as dress ornaments and also for paying shamans for services. Bone cylinders, columellae of shells, and especially polished cylinders of the mineral magnesite were highly prized. These might be used as the central piece of a necklace in the same manner that we might utilize a precious gem.

Chapter XVIII
CEREMONIAL DRESS

All local tribes used the beautiful salmon colored feathers of the Red-shafted Flicker, a woodpecker also known to us by the name Yellowhammer. A headband of the bird's feathers---the stiff quills---was worn on the forehead. Mountain Maidu doctors wore this item also as a belt. In addition Atsugewi made a full feather band which was worn in a variety of ways including hanging down the back. This was usually used only by the shamans.

Another ceremonial item was the California or Acorn Woodpecker scalp headband. This usually had a buckskin strap base, however, mountain Maidu glued these gay feathered patches onto fur bands. Yana wore woodpecker scalps on buckskin as belts.

Mountain Maidu made belts of bands on which the showy greenish feathered neck skins of male Mallard Ducks in mating plumage were strung.

For ceremonial use it was generally customary to tuck small tufts of feathers into the top of the hair. Among Atsugewi, chiefs only used eagle feathers for this purpose. This tribe also fastened single feathers into the crown of buckskin caps in a radiating manner, and also onto strips hanging down the back. Sometimes feathers were tipped with small white feathers to make the former even more decorative. Feathers were also fastened to head nets in a number of ways which differed somewhat among our tribes. Among Atsugewi, women wore these on occasion, but generally it was the males who decked themselves with feathers. Feather plumes of various sorts, employing either twisted buckskin or stick bodies, were also in general use.

Chapter XIX
TOBACCO AND SMOKING

The knowledge and use of tobacco are among the important elements which our own culture of today has inherited from the Indians of North America. Of what benefit this has been is a debatable matter, but its effect has been profound, both on our customs and our economy.

Local tribes used simple one piece wooden pipes of tubular design for the most part in smoking tobacco. Atsugewi and mountain Maidu commonly employed elder and other woods with a pithy and easily removed center. Although not otherwise being considered in this account, the Shasta Indian technique of pipe making is mentioned here because of its uniqueness. These folks hollowed pipe stems by soaking the end of a suitable stick in salmon oil. The larvae of the salmon fly were then introduced, and these wormlike creatures, eating the nourishing fishy core, would bore their ways lenghtwise through the center of the heartwood where most of the salmon oil was concentrated. The Yana habitually used the wood of ash as pipe stock. Mountain Maidu found but did not manufacture a few simple stone pipe bowls also of tubular design. These had considerable spiritual significance and were treated with great care. Garth states that Atsugewi also had short stone pipes, tubular in shape, to which elder or rose wood extensions up to eleven inches in length were applied. Stone pipes were apparently not common in the Lassen region, however.

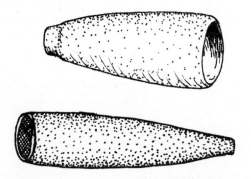

Steatite stone pipes were used without wooden stems, each between three and four inches long. The holes in such pipes were made by tapping a deer antler piece in the depression containing some sand, a slow but effective boring process. This was commonly done by Valley tribes.

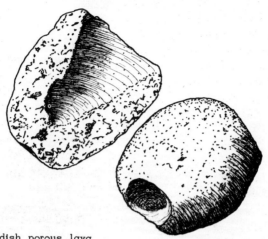

Yana reddish porous lava (dacite?) pipe, broken half, both sides shown. Note funnel - shaped depression in the bottom of the outside (lower half)

Pipes were used at social gatherings, after sweating, and at bed time. The pipes of the local tribes did not have any bends or curves. These straight tubular pipes were therefore most conveniently smoked when the Indians were reclining on their backs thus keeping the tobacco from falling out. Pipes were normally passed around, and used only by the men. However, women shamans of the mountain Maidu also smoked them. Shamans regularly used pipe smoking in ceremonies, especially when healing the sick.

Tobacco grew wild and burning of brush was performed in certain localities to promote the growth of *Nicotiana* plants. Tobacco was not cultivated, but mountain Maidu did collect and scatter seeds in favorable areas. Tobacco was prepared merely by collecting the leaves when fully developed but still green, then drying, preferably in the shade, and finally crumbling the cured leaf in the hand. Tobacco was carried in buckskin pouches usually. Atsugewi often added manzanita and deer grease to their smoking tobacco. Indians of this region did not chew tobacco nor did they eat it with lime as was the custom elsewhere in California. Native tobacco is quite strong.

Chapter XX
MUSIC AND ART

Music of local tribes was limited indeed. It was usually made by men. Only Atsugewi among the Lassen tribes possessed the drum, and this is believed to have been of recent introduction. It was a tambourine type: flat, cylindrical, a foot or so across, and with buckskin shrunken over one end.

The shamans of all tribes used cocoon rattles. These were made of large cocoons from which the moth pupae had been removed through a small hole. Pebbles or seeds were then inserted and usually five or six cocoons---- among Atsugewi as many as thirty ---were tied onto the end of a wooden handle and dried. Cocoon rattles were considered dangerous and were usually kept hidden out of doors, being used by shamans only when doctoring.

A single split stick clapper was employed generally for all types of singing and dancing, not being reserved for any special type of person or ceremony.

Deer-hoof rattles were made from the small hard "dew-claws" from the backs of deer legs. About twenty dew-claws were tied loosely with thongs to a strip of buckskin which was then wrapped about a stick with a plain handle. The deer-hoof rattle was operated by vigorously jerking it lengthwise, in and out. It was used exclusively in the important puberty rites when girls attained womanhood.

Deer - hoof rattle, length about ten inches (after Dixon)

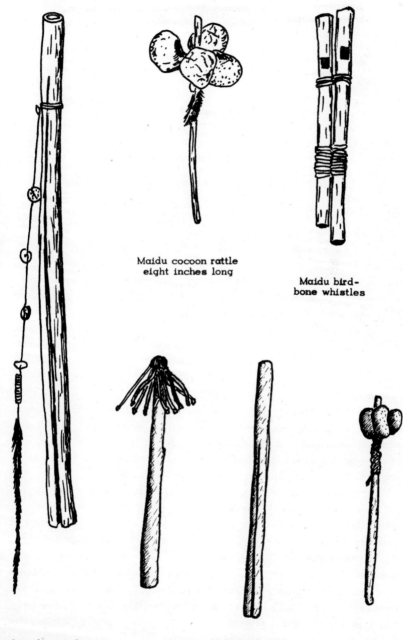

Maidu cocoon rattle
eight inches long

Maidu bird-
bone whistles

Maidu split-stick
clapper, twenty
inches long

Atsugewi deer-
claw rattle

Universal split-
stick dancing
rattle

Maidu
cocoon rattle

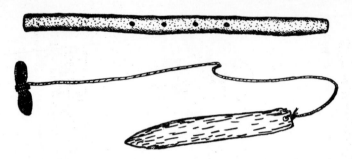

Flute and bull-roarer of local manufacture

Atsugewi and Yana employed hunting bows as musical instruments by holding one end in the mouth and plucking the string with fingers. Mountain Maidu did so too, but like the others only for their own amusement.

Bone, cane, and elder whistles were blown at dances. Flutes, the most tuneful of Indians' instruments, were not played at ceremonies or at dances, curiously enough, but just for self amusement, or in the case of mountain Maidu also for courting pretty girls. Flute melodies were supposed to tell stories, but words were not sung to help the interpretation. Yana made a six-hole flute; other tribes of the Lassen area used a four hole model. In all cases they were open, reedless instruments blown at an angle across one end. The flute was most frequently made of elder wood---mountain Maidu burned the holes into it with live coals.

Except for basketry designs art as such is virtually non-existent. A few simple designs were painted onto hunting bows, and some nose and ear pendants might be considered jewelry art forms, but of the lowest development. The application of face and body paints and tattooing were also simple examples of Indian art.

There appear to be no cliff or cave paintings in the vicinity of Lassen Peak, but they are abundant in Lava Beds National Monument about 75 miles to the north. A different matter is that of petroglyphs which, in California, usually have been made by striking or pecking smooth rock surfaces with small hard stones. Some of these are to be found in the Atsugewi and central Yana territories at lower elevation. However, these symbolic markings were not executed by the local tribes. Atsugewi believe them to have been made by mythological characters. It appears that the petroglyphs must have been made by the predecessors of the Hat Creek and Nozi Indians, for these people claim no knowledge of even the meaning of the rock writings. Shortly before going to press the first petroglyph known to come from the Lassen vicinity was found in the territory of the Southern Yana. The site is one where numerous obsidian chips and arrowpoints have been found on a gently south sloping, open forested portion of Lassen Volcanic National Park headquarters area at an elevation of almost 5000 feet and situated slightly west of the village of Mineral and just north of the north edge of Battle Creek Meadow.

This find on a 10 inch boulder appears to be of ancient origin. The surface has weathered considerably yet not so much that the character of the carving has been altered. It is apparent that the quarter inch deep grooves have been made by rubbing rather than by pecking with hard rocks. This is all the more interesting since the boulder bearing the carving is of a tough hard and site lava. It is indeed unfortunate that the significance of this Butte Creek Meadows petroglyph is unknown. The authorities venture the opinion that the stone may have been used in puberty ceremonies. If so, whether by the Southern Yana or their predecessors we do not know either.

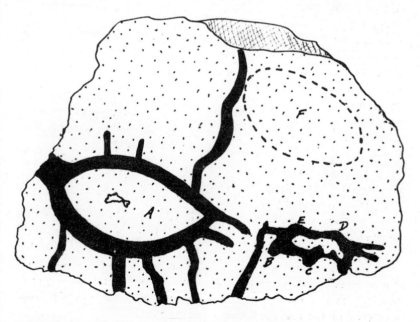

Battle Creek Meadows petrohlyph about nine inches long. The eye-shaped area A is a smooth flat one eighth of an inch below the level of the rest of the rock surface. The grooves bounding it are more than one quarter inch deep and of V-shaped cross-section while the other markings are much shallower troughs with rounded bottoms some being quite vague. B, C, .D, and E indicate deeper rounded depressions. F is a smooth and very uniform slightly concave area.

Chapter XXI
GAMES AND SOCIAL GATHERINGS

Heavy betting on games was the rule. Games were commonly played between neighboring villages or even on occasion with neighboring tribes. Gambling was an important element in these contests and large sums were bet. Sometimes nearly all of a person's or even of a group's possessions were at stake. Evaluation of the stakes in white man's terms is difficult, but they are said frequently to have been of the order of several hundred dollars or even as much as a thousand dollars. Important games lasted more than one day --- perhaps three or four days. The players caught brief rests only and were completely exhausted by the time the playing was over. Singing was the usual accompaniment and high quality rendition at games was much admired. Cheating was rare, maybe because it was supposed to bring subsequent bad luck.

Most games were guessing games. There was considerable variety in the character and number of gambling stones or wooden sticks used, the manner of shuffling and other details. The sticks were shuffled and then concealed in the hands of one or several players on one side. The opposition had to determine the location of the marked stick or the arrangement of several. There were many spectators and excitement ran high. Women occasionally participated along with the men who were the main contestants. Counting sticks might be supplied to each side in equal number at the beginning. More often, however, the sticks were all placed in a common pile at the outset, the successful side taking a counting stick with each win. These scoring sticks were taken and surrendered as the tide of the game changed until one side had all. The game was won at this point.

Ball games were played too. The ball was of buckskin stuffed with hair. The object was to kick the ball between the other team's goal posts. Kicking ball races over given courses and back, or around a lake shore, were also indulged in. In some contests the men and youths on opposing sides would engage in restraining each other so that a number of individual or group wrestling bouts developed on the playing field.

Yana gambling bone, four inches long

There were foot races of distances either short or up to fifteen miles or so in length. Also archery contests and wrestling matches were held. In wrestling the object was to throw the opponent to the ground; tripping was not allowed. Contests in which heavy rocks were tossed, somewhat in the manner of today's shot-put, and heavier rocks carried in competition over a designated line were other games in which the Atsugewi engaged.

Shinny was played by women and children as well as by men, but adult sexes played separately in all of our tribes except Yana. Among them only men participated in this game. Mountain Maidu had three players on a side; Atsugewi had five players. Straight shinny sticks curved at the striking end were used and the puck was a hide affair. Mountain Maidu used a double ball puck. An attempt was made to keep the puck in the air in play. The object, of course, was to get the puck to go between the opponents' goal posts. The Yana used a puck of two bones linked by a string several inches long. Running with the puck on the stick as well as hitting, and throwing it down the field were permitted.

Child's
acorn top

Children improvised a number of games in the same manner as our own children do today in copying their parents. They played house with limbless but dressed dolls, made and used toy bows and arrows, and made sling shots, too. They commonly tried juggling two stones in one hand, spun acorn tops by hand, and in some instances noise makers such as wooden buzzers and bull roarers were used. In play, loud noise was not condoned, however.

Small feasts might occur at any time and were perhaps the most important social gatherings of Atsugewi. They were usually sparked by a temporary abundance of food. Dancing was not included.

Mr. Garth describes the Atsugewi ". . . . grand occasion . . . . held only when a large supply of food had been accumulated, was the bagapi or 'big time'. . . . The chief called a meeting to decide on the date and then sent his people to various places for deer and other foods. Knotted strings (rokuki) with a knot tied for each intervening day before the festival were sent to other villages. By untying a knot each day other chieftans knew when to start for the host's village. The host chief stood on the roof of his earth lodge and welcomed the visitor, calling each chief by name: 'Don't fall down. Step carefully. I'm glad you have come to see me. Don't be in a hurry.' . . . . Toward evening the visitors might give a dance, after which the host chief called everyone to eat. Large baskets containing acorn mush, meat, sunflower seeds, and other foods were placed on the ground. The host proffered baskets of food to each visiting chief who in turn then distributed the food to his people. In winter two tribal groups on opposite sides of the sweat house might have a competitive sweat dance, vying to see which could endure the heat longest. In summer the sweating was usually omitted, and games of chance were begun. In the several days that followed, foot racing, archery, weight lifting, and other contests were indulged in. Large bets were made by opposing sides on the outcome of each contest, and the losing side at the end of the week's festivities often had little property left. Surplus food was divided among the guests before they departed.''

Chapter XXII
DANCES

Mountain Maidu had more dances and more types of dances than other tribes of the Lassen area. Tribes of the Sacramento Valley had many more and more complicated dance ceremonies than ours did.

Mountain Maidu had formalized sweat dances which were performed inside large dwelling lodges at night and were participated in by both sexes. As in the case of Yana, only one man, the leader, sang and hit the central pole rhythmically with a split stick rattle. The dancers performed simultaneously but in one spot until they were exhausted and took a cold swim afterwards.

Of the less ceremonial Atsugewi sweat dance, Garth states:

". . . . Men danced naked except for circlets . . . . of twisted grass around the waist, head and upper arm, and occasionally from one shoulder diagonally across the chest. . . . Three or four lines of black or white paint might be drawn across the chest and upper arm. Women wore a skirt and only a small amount of paint. The dancing took place in the combination sweat, dance, and dwelling house of the chief or head man. . . . The fire was built high with dry mountain mahogany . . . , pine . . . , and sometimes with willow . . . , all woods which burned without much smoke; the ventilator door was closed and the dance began. The one singer sat in a corner and beat time with a split stick rattle. . . . Each of ten or twelve dancers might approach close to the fire to show his ability to endure heat, pick up burning brands, one in each hand, and alternately hit one upper arm and then the other with the brands. The heat often became so intense that water had to be thrown on the center post to prevent its catching fire. There was rivalry to see who could stay inside longest, and after a time one man after another emerged and dived into the icy water nearby or rolled in the snow. There might be sweating three or four nights in succession on the occasion of a communal hunt."

Mountain Maidu held a dance gathering each spring for Black Bear and Grizzly Bear. They believed that this dance had been done by animals in mythical "before Indian times". This gathering lasted three days and nights, but the actual dance was in progress only one day and night. Only women danced but men participated in the ceremony dressed in bear robes. There was much feasting too.

The pre – and post – war dances are discussed under the chapter on war.

Chapter XXIII
POLITICAL ORGANIZATION OF TRIBES

Tribes, as we think of them, were non-existent as political units, and hence there were no tribal chiefs, but there were village chiefs, in the California province.

The self governing unit was always a village or a group of small closely adjacent villages. This is the political unit which was governed by the chief. Villages might consist of from four to about twenty-five earth lodges and bark huts with populations of from twenty-five to a hundred or more persons. Influential leaders, usually of much wealth---but not necessarily so---were recognized as head-men, exercising considerable authority over the smaller villages or separated groups of houses near villages. However the head-man's authority was subservient to that of the chief.

Chieftainship was inherited through the father's lineage, the oldest son being the first in succession. However, if the son were too young to take over, the deceased chief's brother was temporarily in charge. The qualities of good character and knowledge were also important qualifications for chieftainship, and a chief could be deposed if he were not a good one. Tenure was normally for life, dependent upon satisfactory behavior and performance of his responsibilities.

The chief's relatives hunted and fished for him, but he fed visitors and provided most of the food for feasts. The chief always directed community economic activities such as group fishing, deer hunting, and root digging expeditions. For this reason chiefs had to know much about game, fish runs, ripening seasons, et cetera, and had to possess good judgement to insure success of group undertakings. Chiefs also spoke to their people mornings and evenings, and at ceremonies and the like. Chiefs furthermore declared days of rest when chores were done about home. Another function was to arbitrate quarrels among the people.

Mountain Maidu villages had assistant chiefs besides, who were sons or brothers of the chiefs. This assistant advised the chief and substituted for him as the occasion demanded. A specific duty of his was the division of food at ceremonies.

Some chiefs had secondary female chiefs who in the case of the Maidu were daughters, among Atsugewi the chiefs' wives. A woman in this capacity supervised preparation of food for feasts and in Atsugewi villages might give orders to men.

Atsugewi chiefs appointed clowns at ceremonies who were paid.

Appointed messengers were a part of every chief's staff. They were selected on the basis of both willingness to serve and ability. Maidu had about six messengers per village while the number varied among Atsugewi. Messengers were good speakers, reliable men, and were discharged if they failed in their duties. These included not only message running, but among Atsugewi, tending fires at ceremonies. For Maidu chiefs, messengers welcomed guests and traveled about gathering news and scouting. Special fire tenders were appointed in this tribe.

Atsugewi chiefs seem to have possessed greater prestige and authority than those of the mountain Maidu, the Yana, and the Yahi. The decisions of Atsugewi chiefs were final, but these had to be diplomatic if the chief were to remain popular. If a chief were unpopular some of his people would move to another village leaving the first chief's community numerically weaker. Chiefs were generally well obeyed by rich and poor alike. In return, chiefs unfailingly had the interests of their people at heart. Atsugewi chiefs, specifically, set examples of industry, behavior, and judgement for their people. No doubt this was generally true of the chiefs of units in other local tribes too.

Because of the greater popularity, prestige, and consquently larger following of some individual chiefs, they were considerably more powerful than other chiefs in the same tribe. Such men were influential to some extent beyond the boundaries of their own territories.

Chapter XXIV
WAR AND PEACE

Wars were commonly small scale encounters and might be either within tribes or between tribes. Atsugewi were not often agressive. Most tribes at one time or another had differences with neighboring tribes, but friendly relations were usually re-established soon. Certain tribes, however, were repeatedly or traditionally enemies, as for instance, Klamath, Paitue, or Modoc against Atsugewi; Washoe against mountain Maidu; Achomawi or Wintun against the the Yana tribes; and mountain Maidu or Wintun against Yahi. Tribes sometimes helped each other in wars, and either payment or reciprocal aid was usually forthcoming.

Causes of hostilities in the Lassen area were usually revenge for murders (if uncompensated), abduction of women and children, or insults to chiefs. Mountain Maidu, Yana, and Yahi also waged wars on account of poaching, rape, alleged witchcraft, and the like. All able bodied men normally went to war, but mountain Maidu left some at home to protect the women.

Chiefs generally did not participate in the fighting although they often went along on the war expedition. Instead of leading the battles themselves, chiefs appointed special warrior leaders who were principal targets of the opposition. Such battle leaders were often head-men, but always were men competent to lead the fight and who had good arrow dodging power.

Shamans habitually went to war, but did not fight actively except on occasion. They were busy singing during battle and urging the warriors on or exhorting supernatural help. The Atsugewi shaman reportedly "stayed behind a tree all the time giving out his power".

Preparation for war consisted of practicing dodging arrows, shooting arrows, in some cases at effigies, and in dancing. The main purpose of the preparation was to incite enthusiasm for the fight. This was so successful that quite a commotion developed in the community, to the extent that such incidents occurred as warriors with knives chasing women and a man shooting his own dog with an arrow! Preparatory war dances were held outside near the villages. Both men and women participated and shamans sang. Mountain Maidu sustained their dances for several days. Warriors spoke to their arrows addressing them as persons. Atsugewi men painted themselves with white and black stripes on faces, limbs, and bodies. Yana used red and white war paint. Mountain Maidu wore head nets and bands. Dried untanned skins of bear, elk, and such were worn at dances as well as in battle, as were waistcoat armors of strong vertical sticks lashed together. Leather helmets were worn by some warriors.

The enemy was usually attacked just at dawn using the element of surprise to the fullest extent possible. Some battles were pre-arranged in which a number of participants faced each other in well formed lines. Such conflicts were subject to "calling off" if too many men were injured or killed. Serious raids, however, did not give quarter and men, women, and children were killed. Booty was taken and scalps, too, were stripped from fallen victims. Scalps were later burned by Atsugewi, but mountain Maidu dried human scalps on frames. This tribe also took entire heads from bodies on occasion. Prisoners were taken too: Atsugewi not infrequently adopted captured children. Captive women might be mistreated and raped, then killed. Adult prisoners might escape with relative ease because there was no suitable way to confine them permanently, and some were returned voluntarily.

While the war party was away on its expedition, the women at home danced individually in the manner of the war dance. They sang and prayed to help the men at war. Atsugewi women dancers carried feathers, bows, and arrows, but rattles were not used in these morale dances.

Upon return of the war party a victory dance was held in or near the village in the open air. Men and women danced independently, but together at the same time. Atsugewi men painted themselves red and white instead of the black and white used for the pre-war dance. They wore headdresses of all sorts and the warriors carried their bows, arrows, armor, and other fighting gear while dancing. The victory dance took place around a fire. Next to the fire Atsugewi planted a short pole on which the new scalps were displayed while mountain Maidu danced with the scalps secured to hand-carried sticks. It is worth noting that while some readers may consider this gloating over human scalps to be a primitive morbidity, it is true that often white men---the very pioneers we eulogize---took and coveted human scalps themselves.

Warriors, particularly those who had killed adversaries, purified themselves by swimming, rubbing aromatic plants on their bodies, praying for luck. They did not eat meat for from a few to many days, depending on the tribe. Among Atsugewi they also sweated with the same end in view, and women brushed the men's bodies with plant materials to aid the purification process.

Surprisingly, the eating of hot foods and any form of meat was taboo to wounded warriors. This seems strange, since these are the very foods which we consider beneficial to injured persons.

When an attack appeared likely upon an Atsugewi village, the whole population retired to high ground which was easily defended. Such sites were prepared in advance and might be considered crude forts as they were surrounded by rock walls and provided with shelters for the non-combatants.

In intertribal wars there was usually no compensation as such made where the encounter had been motivated by the satisfaction of securing revenge. In the case of feuds or murders within the tribe payment was made to relatives of the slain. If persons on both sides were slain compensation was made for all the dead. The chief or head-man supervised the peace negotiations. Payment was usually in beads or money, but Atsugewi sometimes paid off in women or in the amount of the usual price of a bride. In this tribe too, the amount of compensation was made according to the wealth of the victim. A poor man's life was not considered to be worth as much as a rich man's. Atsugewi had a settlement dance meeting in which both sides were present and wore fighting regalia. These dancers disarmed themselves after the payment had been made.

Chapter XXV
BIRTH AND BABIES

The natural function of birth obviously varied only in details of handling the situation, delivery assistance, disposition of the afterbirth, and methods of cutting and treating the child's umbilical cord. The baby was born in a separate hut which contained a trench heated with coals. These were covered with grass and pine needles or fir boughs. On this warm green bed the woman lay at least a part of the time during labor and also after delivery.

Children were desired and a barren woman was looked down on socially. Inability to produce children was grounds for divorce. The behavior of both p a r e n t s during pregnancy was believed to closely affect personality and health of the child.

After giving birth, the mother remained in isolation for from nearly a week to a month or more. Many taboos were imposed upon her. Bathing in streams and sweat baths, eating fresh or dried meat or fish, grease, and often salt were forbidden to her. Most tribes of the Lassen area also prohibited combing of the mother's hair by herself during the period of isolation. Also taboo was scratching herself with her hands, making baskets, preparing food, or traveling.

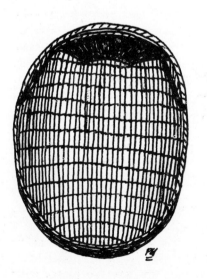

Front and side views of Atsugewi cradle basket for a very young baby.
(tseh - nay - gow)

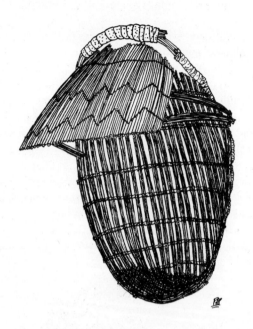

Atsugewi young baby carrying basket or teseh-nay-gow

There were restrictions on the father of the newly born child too. Among Atsugewi and Yana he stayed with the mother, but mountain Maidu fathers stayed away for periods of a week or less. Immediately after the birth had taken place, the father ran to the woods to break up and bring home quantities of fire-wood. Hunting and fishing of all kinds and traveling were taboo for several weeks in most cases. Atsugewi and mountain Maidu new fathers were also forbidden to smoke and gamble, and like their wives, were denied eating fresh or dried fish, meat, and grease for varying periods up to a month. Release from taboos occurred with sweating and bathing among Atsugewi and mountain Maidu. Fathers in these tribes also gave away the first kill when they resumed hunting.

The mother generally massaged the infant to improve the shape and proportion of nose, face, limbs, and torso. Shedding of the baby's umbilical cord was an important event which the Indians wished to occur as soon as possible. A variety of odd practices to this end were employed. The occurrence of the event relieved the parents of some, or in other cases of all, the post birth taboos. Among most of our tribes the dried cord was saved until the child reached manhood or womanhood. It was customarily secured to the cradle basket, but frequently was subsequently lost.   Earlobes

might be pierced in early infancy especially if the child were prone
to cry much.

Two cradle baskets were used. Mountain Maidu made two of
similar oval shape, but the first and smaller one was without a
hood. Atsugewi and Yana tribes made two different types, but both
with rounded carrying handles and sunshades on top. These were
constructed of willow ribs, pine root, and buckskin. The first small
basket was called tseh-nay-gow by Atsugewi and was used for
several months. It was short and with a distinctly rounded basketry
shelf or lip at its lower end. The larger baby basket was called
yah-bih-dee and was practically identical to that of the mountain
Maidu. This was made of the usual twined basketry materials, but
was of different construction. Willow ribs were lashed onto a sturdy
one-piece forked branch frame, the joint being at the bottom. The
base or stem of this Y-piece stuck out below for several inches
being sharpened so that it could be stuck into the ground near the

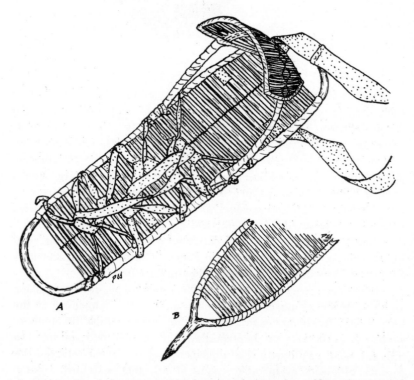

Atsugewi older baby carrying basket or yah-birr-dee. Note the rounded
bottom on A, a modernization. Partial illustration B shows old style construction with a pointed bottom for thrusting into the ground.

Maidu baby carrying basket about thirty five inches long.

mother in camp or when she was out digging roots in the fields. Boo - noo - koo - ee - menorra tells of an interesting modification of the yah - bih - dee today. Its frame is now simply rounded at the bottom instead of having the pointed end described above. "Most people have cars now a days" she says, "and that point poked a hole through the seat of the car. So now we make the round kind." Our visitors to Lassen Volcanic National Park are always interested in names of the "papoose basket". This term and the words moccasin, wampum, and so on are no doubt of Indian origin being the actual words of reasonable facsimilies thereof used. by some eastern tribe for the objects concerned. English speaking Americans have adopted these names as meaning those particular articles for all Indian tribes. It may be recalled that earlier in this book, it was pointed out that each tribe had its own distinct language and so, obviously, each tribe would have had its own distinct names for these objects. Hence there is no all inclusive "Indian name" for the cradle basket or anything else.

The baby was wrapped in tanned buckskin or soft furs, normally wildcat by the Atsugewi. A pad of grass or padded bark was placed on the cradle board or basket and then the child was lashed into the tshe - nay - gow with buckskin straps in a sitting position on the sill with its feet hanging down. Most tribes used dry grass, pounded until soft, for diapers, but mountain Maidu used skin material for the purpose. Babies were kept in the cradle baskets until they were able to walk. The cradle frame was carried on the mother's back with a tump - line passing over her forehead or chest. A series of larger cradle baskets were made as the child grew, usually three before the child was allowed to crawl or walk.

The newborn infant was never fed the colostrum from its mother. The baby was either let go without food or given a cooked meat gruel for nourishment for the first two days or so until bonafide milk was produced in the mother's breasts. Children were nursed as often as they wished and until they were quite large: even three or four years old.

Names were given to children usually at the age of about a year. Yana waited even longer, however, until ages of four to six years before giving real names which for this tribe were habitually of a hereditary nature. In the meantime, temporary descriptive nicknames were given. Many real Atsugewi names had meanings, while those of mountain Maidu and Yana normally did not. Nevertheless, Yana and to a certain extent other Indians too, might acquire additional nicknames and descriptive names later in life, even in adulthood.

Twins were unwanted among all local tribes, probably because of the double care and feeding responsibilities involved. Mountain Maidu thought that twins were bad luck and actually feared them. It was generally believed that twins were caused by the mother having eaten twinned nutmeats. These, therefore, were carefully avoided.

Killing newborn babies whether illegitimate, twins, crippled, or when the mother died in childbirth, was practiced only on very rare occasions. Certainly infanticide was not the rule among any of the local tribes, but of course was practiced in certain other areas.

Yana baby cradle basket for young baby.

Chapter XXVI

ADULTHOOD RITES

A girl's attainment of puberty or womanhood was an event of obvious importance and it was recognized as such by all tribes of the Lassen region with extensive formal ritual and ceremony for each individual girl. Only the more important and generally employed taboos and rites are noted below. There was considerable variation in details of such matters even among the four tribes with which we are dealing.

The girl was secluded in a separate hut for from three to six days and sometimes during the nights too. The taboos she observed during this time were much like those imposed on a mother giving birth, but were even more extensive. The young lady must eat from her own special baskets, not cross streams, avoid contacting men --- especially hunters, refrain from gazing at the sun or moon, et cetera. Among things she must do were to wear a basketry cap, or special head bands among some tribes, and have her hair put up in two knobs wrapped over her shoulders. This had to be done for her as she was not allowed to touch her own hair. Carrying the deer-hoof rattle she must run races with other girls, and dance much also, scratch her head only with a special scratcher, have her earlobes pierced if this had not already been done, and frequently her nose septum was punctured too, being kept open by insertion of a round stick. Among Wintun tribes of the Sacramento Valley some taboos lasted for from one to three years!

For several nights public dances were held which lasted all night. Since there was no special ritual for anyone but the girl for whom the dances were held, these ceremonies were of a joyous nature and were popular and well attended. In the middle of the night food provided by the girl's family was served to all present. Singing with deer-hoof rattle accompaniment was carried on all night. Intimate affairs between couples were not unusual during such dances. During the daytime as well dances were held, but these were of short duration and participated in chiefly by the women of the village. At the end of the ordeal the girl bathed and was given new clothes, ending her taboos.

There was no formal ceremony when boys attained manhood except that the youths were generally sent alone into the neighboring mountains for several days to seek special "powers" to give them skill and luck in certain pursuits such as deer hunting, archery, fighting, shamanism, and the like.

During menstration all women had to observe many taboos too. These included eating alone and living in seclusion. They could eat no meat or fish, fat, or salt, and must not cook. They must avoid sick persons and hunters, and could not scratch themselves except with the scratching stick. At the end of the taboo periods of four or five days, they usually bathed in streams for purification.

Curiously, wives' menstrations had to be observed by their husbands in a number of ways. Most common was prohibition of smoking, and they must eat lightly. Among mountain Maidu the husband could hunt and fish, but could not eat any flesh; among Atsugewi the reverse was true.

Chapter XXVII
MARRIAGE AND DIVORCE

Marriage itself was not formalized with any ceremony. It was common practice for parents to arrange marriages when children were young and these arrangements, which involved some exchange of gifts or payment, were usually honored later. Most other marriages were arranged by parents later when the children had reached maturity and generally these recognized the childrens' wishes. Both of these types of marriages were the basis for extensive exchange of presents and visits, details of which differed among the several tribes. In addition there was almost universal payment for the girl---about ten strings of clamshell disks was standard. The boy and girl became husband and wife simply upon starting to live together, but the new status was usually marked by a feast participated in by the families concerned. Generally there followed a period of residence of the couple with one or both of the in-laws. On occasion marriages grew from intimacies with no parental negotiations, but such matches were not well regarded by the community.

Indian men frequently married women from other villages and occasionally even women from other tribes.

If a wife died her sister was generally obliged to marry the widower. Likewise, if the husband died it was customary that his brother would marry the widow. A wise institution was the relationship of the husband and wife with their in-laws. Neither could speak to nor hand things directly to the in-law of opposite sex, or in some cases even to the brothers and sisters of the in-laws; such things had to be done by a third party. In some instances the mother-in-law even avoided looking at her son-in-law even though she might like him. Such arrangements no doubt prevented many arguments and quarrels, but as far as their own evaluation of these customs were concerned, the basis lay in the belief that a bear might eat either or both of the violators of the in-law taboos.

The practice of having more than one wife at a time was common. One man might have three or four wives, but rarely had more than two at a time. Rich men or head-men and chiefs were most apt to have more than two wives.

Divorce was simple indeed. The man just sent the girl back home if she were barren, lazy, promiscuous, or the like. If he had good reasons for wanting to get rid of his wife, her purchase price might be refunded by her family, or else the ex-wife's sister might be sent to him in exchange, or, sometimes, in addition with no additional payment. On the other hand, the wife might leave her husband if she had been badly mistreated, or if the husband did not provide enough meat and clothing for the family or if he were unfaithful. In divorce the children were divided. Usually, but not always, the girls remained with their mother and the boys with their father. However, divorce was not common among Indians of this region.

On the whole, morals were high and sexual deviations were infrequent, although the whole range of such practices were known to the aborigines. It appears beyond argument that divorces, moral laxity, and sexual aberrations increased with the coming of white man.

Chapter XXVIII
DEATH AND BURIAL

Atsugewi and mountain Maidu left the corpse in the house for
one day. They prepared it for burial by dressing it well and adding
bead necklaces, then wrapping it in a hide. Yana did the same,
washing the body first, and although also adorning the corpse with
jewelry, they always removed decorative nose ornaments, replacing
these with simple sticks. According to Voegelin, Atsugewi removed the body for burial prone and feet first through the wall of
the house, but Garth states that the body was removed through the
southern ventilator passage or through the regular entrance way
in the roof.

The mountain Maidu, Yana, Yahi, and usually the Atsugewi bent
the body into a position called flexed. The arms were folded across
the chest and the knees were drawn up against the stomach before
wrapping the corpse in a robe which was then sewn shut. The
mountain Maidu sometimes put the wrapped cadaver into a large
basket. Voegelin was of the opinion that Atsugewi buried their
dead lying flat on their backs, and if so, always with the head toward the east. It is thought that this prone burial might be a
recent innovation learned from white man.

Mourners among all of our local tribes wailed aloud and brought
gifts for the dead. Women, especially the older ones, mourned
vigorously. To quote Garth again on Atsugewi, of their mourning
he states:

"The deceased's close relatives mourned the hardest, but
friends might also mourn---- 'to make them feel better.'
Mourners cried and rolled on the ground, throwing dirt and hot
ashes in their faces and hair. Some, in their grief, tried to
commit suicide, and a close watch had to be kept over them
to prevent their doing so. Favorite methods were to swallow
small bits of (obsidian) or to eat a certain kind of spider.
Mourners were warned not to cry around the house near the
body but to go to the hills to cry, and also not to look down
when crying or to cry too much. Otherwise they were subject
to bad dreams in which spirits would plague them and possibly
kill them. A mourner might acquire power at this time. A
widow, with possibly a sister to help her, would wail for a
time at daybreak and again in the evening. This lasted for
two or three months, sometimes longer. A widower seldom
cried more than two or three weeks. The widow visited places

at which she had camped with her husband, broke up utensils
left there, burned down the brush where he was accustomed
to cut wood, and piled up rocks where they had slept together.
A widower behaved in similar fashion....If death occurred in
a village, no entertainments could be held for a time; otherwise relatives of the deceased had the right to break things
up and throw them around. A man would not sing or attend a
'big time' gathering until at least a year after death of a close
relative.''

If the lodge were to be lived in again, after a person had died
in it, Atsugewi brought in juniper boughs, and these were burned
to purify the house. Bark huts, however, were always burned down
after an occupant had died.

Mountain Maidu children were kept away from the dead and from
the funeral proceedings. In that tribe and probably among all local
tribes, if the deceased were rich the funeral would be much larger
and more pretentious than if the person had been poor. In the
former case the ceremony was followed by a feast. Other tribes
buried the dead in the evening generally within twenty-four hours
after death, but Yana waited three or four days. Mountain Maidu
grave diggers put grass in their mouths. Small shallow graves
sufficed for poor people, in fact, among Atsugewi, at least, poor
people were often buried in small depressions in lava flows and
covered over with convenient rocks.

Enroute to Atsugewi burials no one was permitted to look back,
and water was sprinkled along the path to prevent the dead person's
spirit from returning to the village. At the grave the dead were
asked aloud please not to look back, for if they did other members
of their families would die soon.

Cremation, that is, burning of corpses was rare among tribes of
the Lassen area. At the battlefield and in other instances of death
far from home, especially in the case of mountain Maidu, burning
was done occasionally. After this the bones were collected,
wrapped in buckskin, and then buried.

The flexed bodies of the dead were always placed in graves
facing eastward. Widows customarily attempted to throw themselves into the graves, but were restrained from doing so. A basket
of water was invariably placed next to the body, and most personal
property of the deceased was broken and also placed in the grave.
The amount of property so disposed of varied with the tribe.
Mountain Maidu and especially the Yana tribes put practically everything in the grave. The latter even went so far as to include many

gifts of a nature not normally associated with the sex. Aprons and baskets, for instance, might be placed in a man's burial. Among Atsugewi the relatives retained some of the property of the deceased. Atsugewi might place some food on the grave and mark it with a vertical stick, but it was not tended later, and the site was generally soon lost.

In winter a person might be buried shallowly in the floor of a living house. Next spring the house would be torn down and the dirt walls caved in. There was variation not only between, but within tribes as to the final disposition of houses of the deceased. They might be burned down, a common practice, or they were torn down, abandoned, temporarily deserted, or torn down and rebuilt. If to be lived in again, purification of some sort was always practiced, either by burning juniper boughs in the house, smoking tobacco, bringing in aromatic plants, or treating the main beams. Among Yana tribes the family seems to have habitually abandoned the house right after the funeral and to have burned the whole thing including property and food of all the inmates, retaining only the barest necessities of life such as sleeping robes.

Among Atsugewi all mourners had to deny themselves meat and fresh fish for one day; then they sweated and swam after the funeral. Mountain Maidu mourners, including all persons who had had any part in the funeral, had to undergo four or five days taboo on eating all flesh. They also had to eat alone and from separate dishes, do head scratching with special sticks only, were allowed no hunting, gambling, intercourse, or smoking. Purification of those persons contaminated by participation in burial included swimming and washing every day that the taboos were in effect.

Only Atsugewi, of all local tribes, are said to have practiced suicide, though unquestionably it did occur on occasion among all California Indians.

Mentioning the name of the deceased in the presence of his relatives was considered very poor taste, and was actually forbidden in some cases.

It was forbidden that the widow touch the corpse, so that relatives had to prepare the body for burial. After the funeral, the widow always cut her hair off closely. If an Atsugewi, she made a belt out of it, and the hair belt was then often decorated with shells. In all local tribes the widow traditionally covered her whole head and face with pitch and covered this with white diatomaceous earth or black charcoal. Touching her head or face (the whole body for mountain Maidu) with fingers was taboo; she could do this only with the scratching stick which mountain Maidu widows wore around the neck. Raggedy, ill-looking clothes were worn by the survivor, and Atsugewi widows put pitch on old basketry caps to be worn. A mourning necklace was worn at all times, made of lumps of hard pitch strung onto a fiber string. This was worn until remarriage, which was usually two or three years for Atsugewi and one to three years for mountain Maidu. Pitch on the face and head was normally left on until it wore off of its own accord.

The mourning conduct of grieving men who had lost their wives in death was not nearly so lengthy or as rigorous as was that of widows. Widowers cut their hair too, but among Atsugewi the only other observance required was abstinence of flesh eating for a day. Mountain Maidu widowers spent one sleepless night out in the mountains. Widowers did not generally sing at dances and at "big times" for about a year, but this was not compulsory. The Yana are said to have stayed away from dances for two or three years.

Parents mourning the loss of children cut their hair slightly and placed some pitch on hair or faces. The Atsugewi mother observed a three day meat taboo and the Maidu father went to the hills to seek power. However, loss of a baby in birth or before its navel cord dropped off was considered a more serious situation. Such bereaved parents gave all of their belongings away in order to make a fresh start.

Anniversary mourning rites were not conducted in the Lassen region. An exception was the rare instance among Atsugewi when a child was sick at a time just three years after the death of its parent. Under such circumstances a shaman sang over the child and the whole remaining family and relatives mourned, later washing themselves. With respect to the general lack of mourning anniversaries it is of interest that the foothill (northeast) Maidu held elaborate annual burnings for several years after death of relatives. At these great mourning dance ceremonies large quantities of valuable possessions were burned as sacrifices to honor the dead.

Chapter XXIX
COUNTING, TIME, AND PLACE

Counting on the fingers was usual practice. Mountain Maidu started with their thumbs while Atsugewi began on the little finger of one hand and counted across to that on the other hand, and toes were used for the purpose too. To help in counting, tribes also employed sticks to represent groups of numbers: Atsugewi used sticks to represent 1's, 5's, 10's, and hundreds. Yana frequently used a stick to represent the unit 20. This is presumed to be a natural unit because it is the sum of all of a person's fingers and toes.

Time of day, of course, was not expressed in any unit like our hour, but roughly by the position of the sun in its daily course overhead. Seven to nine positions were referred to descriptively in this respect plus early, mid, and late night.

Phases of the moon were most practical and were universally used as a longer measure of time. The succession of new moon cycles were named and an old man in the village customarily kept track of these by memory. As might be expected from this system, in which there was no recording, arguments ensued over just which moon or "month" was currently in effect. One full course of the moon's phases takes just about a month, so the names for Indians' moons corresponded nearly to our month names.

All local tribes recognized four seasons. These were identified by the positions of certain stars among mountain Maidu, but more generally by the positions of the rising sun with respect to a certain peak, tree, or similar fixed object. Some Indians kept track of the seasons by watching the daily progression of a beam of sunlight coming through the smoke hole of a house and falling upon its floor or wall. The shortest day of the year naturally was marked by the most southerly progression of the sun. This was noted by the Indians, no doubt with joy in the realization that longer days and, somewhat later, warmer weather were to be expected. The year started with the beginning of November when Indians of the Lassen area had left the high elevation hunting grounds on the flanks of Lassen Peak, had collected their stores of acorn and salmon, and were warmly settled in their winter quarters. Mountain Maidu seem to have used names for only the nine moons most important to them.

There was no calendar as such, but the number of days until a certain "big time" or other event was kept track of by either cutting off or untying one knot in a knotted cord or thong each day. Years were not recorded either, but were measured within the memory span as so many winters ago, or by relating time to some important event, such as a war which most persons might remember.

Directions were pointed out, or in speech were referred to as sunrise and sunset for east and west respectively. Directions were commonly given with respect to features of the local geography: in the direction of such and such a village or toward a named river, spring, or mountain which was conspicuous or generally known. We must remember that the territories of our local tribes were small and that the terrain was intimately known. Specific names were not only given to the conspicuous features of the topography, but among Atsugewi, at least, virtually every flat, every draw, and every hill was specifically named, and these names were known to all members of the tribe. Names of places in the territories of other tribes were not known by the local names of those tribes. They were either translated or given its own entirely different set of names by the first tribe. In other words, each tribe had different names for all places---a very confusing situation. Dixon reports that Maidu recognized directions as we know them, but that the northeast or mountain Maidu had five: west, northwest (the direction of Lassen Peak), north, east, and south.

Chapter XXX
CONCEPTS OF SUN, MOON, AND STARS

Mountain Maidu and Atsugewi believed the sun to be a female human---the wife---and the moon to be a male human---the husband. This is a reversal of the sex ascribed to these bodies by some other tribes. They believed that the figure of a frog was visible in the moon.

Atsugewi stated that Frog fought Moon and swallowed him and the next time that Moon swallowed Frog who is now in the center of the moon. When Moon and Frog fought, the former was not round, but crescent shaped. Yana stated that in the moon they could see Moon's wife, Frog. Pine Marten snapped his evil father-in-law Moon into the sky by means of bending a springy tree 'way down and suddenly letting it go. He used the same system to snap Frog and her two daughters into the sky also.

To Atsugewi, as to most tribes, the phases of the moon: new, full, and waning, represented birth, life, and death---repeated every four weeks, although, of course, none of the Indians had the concept of a "week" such as we have. All through the year Atsugewi greeted the new moon. Old persons shook themselves, and their clothes and bedding in its presence. Younger folks ran and jumped toward the moon. If the points or horns of the new moon crescent were vertical it was a bad omen indicating sickness or death. Babies were shown the new moon, and in the case of both Atsugewi and mountain Maidu, babies' faces and arms were rubbed in the new moonlight to make them grow fast. All local tribes addressed the moon aloud in friendly terms as if it were a personal relative. The Yana prayed to it. In contrast to Atsugewi reaction to vertical position of the two moon points, the Yana and mountain Maidu accepted this as meaning good fortune and good weather ahead. To these tribes horizontal position of the moon crescent in the winter sky denoted that it was full of water and indicated pending rains or storms. At other seasons both horns up foretold of death. Yana thought that both sun and moon were feminine.

After its daily trip across the sky, Atsugewi thought that the sun returned to the east in a blue cloud via the side of the earth. As the sun and the moon passed each other at the side of the earth, they decided on the weather for the following day. The moon supplied the cold and the sun the heat.

Eclipses of sun and moon were believed by Yana to be due to their dogs devouring them. Atsugewi and mountain Maidu felt that the heavenly bodies were dying. The former were of the opinion that Lizard was eating Sun or Moon as the case might be. They shouted loudly, shot arrows into the air toward the eclipse and beat all available female dogs. Mountain Maidu thought that Frog was eating Moon or Sun.

A reddish moon foretold of disaster and was a sign of war for Atsugewi, but to Yana it meant hot weather ahead.

Only a few star groups of the night sky were named.

Yana thought the constellation we call the Belt of Orion was Coyote's arrow. All local tribes believed the Milky Way to be a road, or river in some cases, which was traveled by departing spirits or souls of the dead. Shooting or Falling stars, (more properly meteorites) presaged good weather to the Atsugewi who thought these were torches carried by spirits from one house to another in the sky. For this tribe too, a single conspicuous star---no doubt a planet---seen near the moon was an evil sign. If the star were on the left someone nearby would die soon; if it lay to the right of the moon someone farther away was doomed.

Atsugewi called the Seven Sisters wir-etisu. These girls were seduced by a little rabbit boy at a puberty dance. They became ashamed and went up in the sky to become stars. The Big Dipper was called Coyote's Cane. Maidu thought that stars were made of something soft like buckskin.

Chapter XXXI
WEATHER PHENOMENA

As mentioned in the preceding chapter, weather was determined by agreement between sun and moon, but it appears that many things could influence their decisions.

Atsugewi assumed it to be the natural thing that it would sprinkle a little after a funeral. They also felt that rolling rocks down mountain sides or loud shouting in the mountains would cause rain. Furthermore they believed that the occurrence of precipitation could be influenced by shamans, if they felt like it, by smoking tobacco while looking at the sun. The nature of the spirit of a girl, whose ears were pierced at this time, was also thought to either cause it to rain or to stop doing so according to her spirit power.

Rainbows brought good wild crops as far as the Atsugewi were concerned. However, both they and mountain Maidu were of the opinion that pointing with a finger at a rainbow, particularly among children would cause the finger to become crooked or to fall off.

Thunder and lightning were feared by all tribes of the Lassen region. To Atsugewi thunder was the shouting of an old man who wears a rabbit skin and who goes about looking for women whom he kills. Mountain Maidu thought it to be due to an old man who lives up above and who was once a boy on earth, but who had been sent away because he was too fast and ate everything in sight. How he made the noise we do not know.

Also, according to Dixon, "Thunder is thought to be a man or boy of miraculous abilities. He eats trees chiefly. Had it not been for Mosquito, however, Thunder would have preyed on people. Mosquito deceived him, and refused to let Thunder know whence the blood and meat he brought came. Had Thunder found out that Mosquito obtained these from people, they, and not the trees, would have been his prey." To Yana, thunder was a mythical dog originally: ". . . . a child dug from the ground who accompanied Flint Boy to the west in the guise of a dog. He remained behind in the black storm clouds capping Bally Mountain, a high peak west of Redding, whence his terrific bark could be heard as thunder."

Atsugewi and mountain Maidu, fearing thunder and lightning, talked to them and told them to go away. Old men in the latter tribe carried burning sticks in a circle to help drive them away. Atsugewi placed skins, preferably raccoon, on sticks held up in the air. They would wave these around and call aloud words to the effect that

there are: "Too many rattlesnakes here, go some other place!".
Not only that, but frequently during a thunder storm, especially if
violent, they would run into open areas, and sometimes even jump
into water. Lightning was thought to be the weapon of the old man,
Thunder Person, mentioned above. It came out of his mouth. Apparently Thunder Person was thought to assume the form of a
raccoon on occasion. Maidu also believed that it would thunder
whenever a person was bitten by a rattlesnake or when a great man
died or when a woman had a miscarriage.

Whirlwinds were generally regarded as evil omens which sickened
people with bad dreams and captured peoples' shadows or spirits.
Indians tried to dodge or hide from them. They spoke informally to
whirlwinds. Mountain Maidu said that they put pains into people.
Whenever possible, Maidu smoked tobacco when talking to whirlwinds. Atsugewi threw dirt and water at the dust devils in an effort
to destroy them. Yana did likewise, but they did not believe that
spirits were inside of whirlwinds.

Chapter XXXII
EARTHQUAKE BELIEFS

Lassen Peak and its vicinity are subject to many local earthquakes today. The geologic nature of the area indicates that this has been so for thousands of years. Lassen Peak was known to the Atsugewi as Wicuhirdiki, which has no meaning. The area was thought to be inhabited by a powerful spirit, but Garth notes that there seemed to be no fear about hunting and fishing there, and the Indians apparently utilized the hot springs medicinally. Garth recorded one pertinent bit of Atsugewi (Apwaruge) myth as follows:

"There once was an earthquake that shook this country up and made those boulders out on the flat shake. It shook so much that it made people sick. There was a very old woman whose hair was almost green. She picked up a rock and pounded it on another rock while she sang. She was praying for the world to stop shaking. Soon she got an answer, and the shaking ceased. Many people were killed. Those who lived in canyons were covered by rocks that were shaken down."

Yana interpretation of the perplexing and frightening phenomenon of earthquakes is tied in, as we might expect, with mythology as follows, to quote from Sapir and Spier:

"A series of fabulous malignant beings were conceived as dwelling in certain localities. In the Sacramento River were water grizzlies (hat-en-na) which pulled fishermen down to devour (them). . . . They were spotted black and white, like dogs. Somewhere (not specified) was a serpent (e-k-u) which killed people. Near Terry's mill were believed to dwell malignant little beings (yo-yautsgi), like little children. They often enticed people and ate them up. At a a marshy spot and spring on Round Mountain, called Ha-mupdi (?), dwelled a being called Mo-s-ugi-yauna who caused the ground to shake when he was displeased.

"Once Mo-s-ugi-yauna made a little baby of himself and put himself in the road of two women. One of them took it up and in sport gave it one of her nipples to suck, though she was really without milk. The baby kept sucking until the girl tried to take her breast away, but without success. The baby kept sucking at her, sucked up her flesh, and at last sucked up her whole body.

"This being was displeased if strangers came near and

talked anything but Yana. Once some Yreka Indians came
and talked Chinook jargon at that place, whereupon the earth
began to shake violently. At last the owner of the place
cried out to Mo - s - ugi - yauna that it was not he who had thus
spoken and begged him 'in the doctor way' to stop, whereupon he did."

Chapter XXXIII
CREATION BELIEFS AND OTHER LEGENDS

All local Indians believed in a mythical age when animals were persons and talked to each other. Both Atsugewi and mountain Maidu thought that floods played a part in the past scheme of things before people were created by gifted animal ancestors.

Garth relates that "Atsugewi mythology tells of the successive creation of two former worlds, the first of which was destroyed by a great flood and the second by a fire which Coyote instigated in an attempt to kill his rival, Grey Fox. After this both Coyote and Grey Fox descended from the heavens on a long rope to the primeval sea below. Here Grey Fox took combings from his fur (in some accounts a piece of sod) and proceeded to make land of it, stretching it to all sides until the present earth was made, in concept a large island floating in the sea. Grey Fox then created trees, animals, and finally people. The sun and moon were two brothers whom Grey Fox told to mount into the sky to light the world, the one during the day and the other at night. . . . Grey Fox first wanted to create two moons and two suns, but Coyote objected saying that it would be too hot. Grey Fox then made only the sun and one moon."

In a somewhat different version, Dixon has recorded that the Atsugewi "....recount how, in the beginning, there was only the illimitable sea and the cloudless sky. Slowly in the sky a tiny cloud began to form, and grew till it reached considerable proportions. Then gradually it condensed, and, becoming solid, became the Silver-Gray Fox, the Creator. Then arose immediately a fog; and from this, as it condensed, and coagulated as it were, arose Coyote. By a process of long-continued and intense thought, the Creator created a canoe into which both he and Coyote descended, and for long years floated and drifted aimlessly therein, till, the canoe having become moss-grown and decayed, they had, perforce, to consider the necessity of creating a world whereon they might take refuge."

The Yana legends quoted below from Gifford and Klimek (first) and from Sapir and Spier are from the northern and central tribes, of that people. These legends are given in lieu of those of southern Yana and Yahi, with which this book should be concerned, because of the similarity of the culture of these four tribes. It is extremely unlikely that there would be very great differences in their legends and beliefs of creation. Obviously each tribe had its own unique details.

North Yana: "Coyote, assistant creator, was marplot (the evil schemer) who brought death into the world as follows: Coyote, his two sons, and other people went down-stream to get clamshells. The people played. Coyote's sons seized the clamshells and ran off with them. One escaped with the stolen shells, but the other was killed. The Coyote boy who escaped shouted to Old Man Coyote, who sat in his assembly house and observed daily what transpired. Coyote boy told the old man his brother was dead. Old Coyote then mourned for his son. Silver Fox told him not to cry, but to clean the assembly house and bring in the dead boy. They strewed the floor with straw and built fire. Silver Fox told old Coyote to lie down and pretend to sleep. 'Do not move,' said Silver Fox. This was to cause dead boy to revive. They started to cut old Coyote's belly to get back the spirit of his dead son. Old Coyote shouted with pain and said: 'Let him stay dead. The dead shall remain dead.' Thus he spoiled Silver Fox's plan for resurrection."

Central Yana: ". . . . the creation of people took place at Wama-riwi, a village at the cove north of Battle Creek and several miles west of the present Shingletown, that is, roughly at the center of Yana territory. Here in the beginning were Lizard and Cottontail (in Dixon's version, Lizard, Gray Squirrel, and Coyote; in Curtin's, Silkworm) who had no predecessors. Discussing how people shall be made, Lizard lays down sticks which they carry to the four directions to become neighboring Indian tribes. Realizing that they have omitted those at the center, they put down bad (short) sticks there. Hence the Yana are shorter than any of their neighbors: a view held by the Yana and repeated by Powers as fact. In Dixon's version (from the same informant) Lizard carefully prepares three sticks for Atsugewi, Wintun, and Achomawi, and as an afterthought, short sticks for the Yana. The first three are placed to the east, west, and north; the others are boiled to transform them into humans. Coyote refuses to recognize them until they speak properly, that is, the Yana tongue. Curtin's version is quite different, although still the Yana are created from sticks: his presumably Northern Yana informant, himself a chief, placed the locale in his own country, at Round Mountain. Here Silkworm puts down three sticks, for the Yana chief, a woman, and an orphan, and a large number around the first for common people; he instructs them how to procure food and admonishes that they obey the chief.

"The origin of sex, or rather its proper attribution rests in the circumstance that in the beginning, women were men; men were women. The women were such poor hunters that people starved. To remedy this, Cottontail placed stones in a fire; when the women were seated, the stones burst, cutting their proper organs, and the women became men. Hands were then webbed like Lizard's. In order that they might handle bows and pestles, Lizard, experimenting, cut his fingers apart. With this as a model, he separated those of humans. (In Curtin's version, Water Lizard remedies the defect for himself alone.) In the beginning when people died, they rose from their graves again. Coyote, who objected to these improvements of human affairs, not only proposes that they shall stay dead but stamps down a dead man who would rise. When his own son dies, he changes his mind, but Lizard, Cottontail, and Gray Squirrel will have none of it, so that death and mourning were established forever."

Again Garth is here quoted on Atsugei beliefs: "As in most of northern California there are numerous natural phenomena in Atsugewi territory which marked some mythological event. A low cone-like rock in Dixie Valley was said to be a basket belonging to Coyote. About four miles south of Pittville on the old village site of Mawakasui was an oblong rock ten feet or so in length which was said to be the petrified remains of a lizard whom Butterfly had killed. The extremely rough tongue of lava-covered land extending down the center of Hat Creek Valley was created by Porcupine to impede Coyote with whom Porcupine was running a race. Eagle Lake was said to have been formerly in Atsuge territory, but Coyote tired of the manzanita berries and camass roots which the people fed to him here, so he moved the lake to the Apwaruge country. Here the people fed him epos roots and treated him better."

The Maidu concept of the world according to Dixon is that of ". . . . floating on the surface of a great sea, but anchored by five ropes stretched by the Creator, which hold the island steady, and prevent it from drifting about. Occasionally some being seizes these ropes and shakes them, and this causes earthquakes. The world was flat when first made from the bit of mud brought up from the depths of the primeval sea by the turtle (turtle does not appear in the northeast or mountain Maidu version) or from the robin's nest floating in the sea. Later the Creator and the Coyote went about over the world, making the rivers and mountains. Coyote was in general responsible for the latter, and for the extreme roughness of the country. . . ." The Creator's stone canoe is said to be visible today on top of Keddie Peak just north of Indian Valley (Greenville); also his and Coyote's dance houses may be seen as huge circular depressions at what is now Durham (near Chico).

In his extensive collection of Maidu myths, Dixon observes that "Throughout the myths there is nowhere any suggestion that the Maidu had any knowledge of any other region, that they were immigrants in the land where they live. This complete absence of any migration tradition is a feature which is very characteristic, and serves to differentiate the mythology not only of the Maidu, but of most Californian tribes, from that of the Southwest, and much of the eastern portion of the continent."

He further states: "here the creation is a real beginning: beyond it, there is nothing. In the beginning was only the great sea, calm and unlimited, to which, down from the clear sky, the Creator came, or on which he and Coyote were floating in a canoe. Of the origin of previous place of abode of either Creator or Coyote, the Maidu know nothing. . . . "

". . . . the whole series of tales told by the stock . . . . appeared to follow one another in a more or less regular and recognized order. Beginning with the creation, a rather systematic chain of events leads up to the appearance of the ancestors of the present Indians, with whose coming the mythic cycle came to a close. This mythic era, the be-be-ito, seems to fall into a number of periods, with each of which a group or set of myths has to deal. First, we have the coming of Ko-do-yan-pe (Earth-Namer or Creator) and Coyote, their discovery of this world, and the preparation of it for the 'first people'; next the creation of these first people, and the making and planting of the germs of the human race, the Indians, who were to come after; third, the long period during which the first people were in conflict, and were in the end changed to the various animals in the present world. In this period Earth-Maker tries to put an end to Coyote, whose evil ways and wishes are in direct contrast to his own" Creator was always dignified and striving to make life easy, happy, and deathless for mankind, while Coyote, a trickster and amorous knave, worked with continued success to render life difficult for man with the result that man's lot is to suffer and finally to die. This belief was generally uniform among the tribes of the Lassen area. ". . . . During this period Earth-Maker strives for a last time in vain with Coyote, his defeat, and disappearance toward the East coincident with the appearance of the human race, which bursts forth from the spots where the original pairs had been buried long before." These potential human beings had been made ". . . . as tiny wooden figures by the Creator, and planted here and there in pairs, that they might grow in secret and safety during the time of monsters and great conflicts. . . ."

In other myths also there is great similarity among the Maidu, Atsugewi, Yana, and Yahi. Dixon says concerning ". . . . The theft of fire, for instance. . . . In all, the fire is held by a man and his daughters, and is discovered largely through the agency of the Lizard; the fire is watched and guarded by a sentinel bird, is stolen in consequence of his sleeping while on guard, and pursuit by the women is hindered by the strings of their skirts being cut as they sleep. The fire is brought back by a group of animals, among whom the fire is divided for safety; and the pursuers, who are usually Thunder, and his two daughters Rain and Hail, are put to flight."

Chapter XXXIV
MEDICAL TREATMENT

The bulk of the important doctoring was done by shamans or medicine men. This was all based on supernatural faith and fear. As we know from advances of our modern civilization in the field of psychosomatic medicine, such "in the mind" cures were highly effective in practice. With all due respect to the modern medical profession, it is a foregone conclusion that from 50% to 75% of the patients of today's general medical doctor are going to get well eventually without any bonafide medical treatment anyway. This percentage favored the shamans too.

Besides shamans there were secondary Indian doctors called herbalists. Among Atsugewi, these persons did not have the power of shamans, and could not cure disease, but only check or weaken it. However, this class of doctor did administer various medicines internally and externally, and gave treatments which may actually have been--- in some cases --- of benefit beyond mere faith healing. These remedies were handed down, as was all Indian knowledge, by word of mouth from generation to generation. Old men taught the young.

Herbalists were able to make snake bite victims recover; treatment included sucking the wound. Cauterization or burning of affected parts was practiced. Atsugewi treated rheumatism in patients with vapor baths in a trench of hot coals on which pine needles and yerba santa or mountain balm branches were placed, with a robe over all.

Mountain Maidu smoked wild parsnip for headaches, colds, and wounds. Mountain Maidu and Atsugewi believed that toothaches were caused by the presence of worms in the teeth. Corrective poultices were placed on the cheek. Yana did this too, but placed a hot stone on the poultice, and also bit on a mole's front foot, dried, to relieve the pain. Atsugewi often set the poultice on fire which might leave permanent scars.

The seeds of rosinweed, a member of the sunflower family, were collected, then shelled, cooked, dried, and finally pounded. This medicine was taken for chills. Wild iris roots were chewed raw for coughing.

Decoctions, that is, water in which plants had been boiled to extract their medicinal juices, were drunk. California angelica, a member of the parsley family, was used in this way for colds, diarrhea, headache, et cetera. This medication was popular with all local tribes for treating many ills.

Yana used poultices of roots of bracken fern, pounded and warmed for application to burns. The bulbs of false solomon seal were pounded fine and also hot soap-root poultices were applied to swellings, pains, or boils. Peeled California angelica roots were crushed and laid on aching heads.

Ground squirrel grease was used to soften rough hands and to relieve cracking of the skin from chapping.

Atsugewi employed green leaves of chokecherry, pounded as poultices, for cuts, sores, and bruises. The boiled liquor of pounded chokecherry bark was used for bathing wounds to promote healing.

They employed decoctions of wormwood to prevent blood poisoning and to treat cuts. Decoctions of greenleaf manzanita leaves were good for cuts and burns. Both oak bark and oak gall decoctions were drunk to prevent infection and catching colds and were given to women in childbirth. Atsugewi also chewed raw juniper berries as a treatment for colds.

Obviously there was a host of other treatments as we know of a large variety of other plants, roots, and fruits which were used medicinally.

Broken bones were set as best they could be set, and were bound up in simple but effective splints.

For general good health Garth states that an Atsugewi "…. man chewed the top shoot off a young pine tree. Especially was this done by a father after his wife bore a child."

In Yana sweat houses and probably in those of other tribes too, veins were cut with obsidian chips to "let the bad blood out" if a person felt ill.

Chapter XXXV
SPIRITS AND GHOSTS

Ghosts and spirits were one and the same, and were to local Indians as souls are conceived by white man, yet the Indian conception was more variable. Some spirits were good and others were evil, but all were feared and avoided whenever possible. They were frequently associated with omens and had somewhat the appearance of human beings. Among Atsugewi they were visible only to shamans, but were heard by nearly all persons. Yana commoners both saw and heard spirits, but only very rarely.

The spirit left the body right after death. Mountain Maidu thought that it turned back once before going on. Yana believed that the spirit tarried in the vicinity of the body for a while, going to the south first briefly for a sort of trial or evaluation which included determination as to whether or not the nose septem had been pierced. Then, as all local Indians apparently agreed, the ghost or spirit went to a distant place in the west via the Milky Way. Yana thought that there was some distinction in destination of good and bad persons' ghosts, but our other tribes conceived only of one place for all spirits finally. We do not today have a very clear understanding of the aboriginal Indian concept of heaven except that people lived in this land of the dead in sweat houses, hunting, eating, loving, and sleeping, but with complete absence of sickness. Concepts of the life of spirits changed with the coming of the whites preceding even the advent of pioneer settler days. All information in that regard which students have been able to gain from informants in this region is decidedly flavored with Christian dogma.

Spirits or ghosts returned to old haunts of the body on occasion or, more often, to the vicinity of the grave. For this reason burial grounds were usually well removed from villages. Bad smells would drive spirits away, while whistling and flowers attracted them. Fiber-wound crossed sticks were hung in sweat houses of Yana tribes to keep spirits out. All tribes of the Lassen area thought that ghosts visited the living in dreams and also considered it feasible that the spirits of people might go to visit those of the dead when the persons were asleep, or more commonly when the living were unconscious.

Mountain Maidu didn't speak much about ghosts, but if one had been making a nuisance of itself by visiting much in dreams, they fed it by having all members of the family throw small portions of food into the fire before commencing to eat their meals. Besides, a shaman was hired under these circumstances to sing for the dreamer. The same ceremony was observed by the Atsugewi. It was also the practice of the dreamer in this tribe to eat with a dog, spitting out some of the food, saying to the dog, "You better eat for me. Take that spirit away". Atsugewi were evidently very conscious of ghosts for they spoke to them, spit out chewed epos roots for the spirits, smoked tobacco for them, burned hair and skin to repel them, and tobacco and feather bundles were hung near the house doorways for their benefit. New Atsugewi parents had a unique ritual at the time of their first meat eating after the taboos of childbirth---they chewed small amounts of meat and put this on their toes for the dogs to eat.

Garth says of Atsugewi spirit beliefs: "A man who was about to die, whether he felt sick or not, had a peculiar ordor about him. If he went hunting, deer ran from him saying, 'Phew, that man smells bad.' Coyotes and dogs would come close to him and bark at him. He would die unless a shaman could remove this aura of death from him."

There were many omens of a spirit nature which foretold calamity. To Atsugewi upon hearing the cries of certain animals at night, especially if an owl hooted at one, or if one saw a kingsnake, death was supposed to descend upon a relative.

If evil spirits frightened a person and tried to steal his soul, the spirits could be foiled by standing with one's feet widely spread apart. If followed by a ghost, a person might turn around, retracing his footsteps while the spirit continued in the direction one had been traveling initially.

When a person was asleep his spirit could wander around. If, during these wanderings, a bad spirit caught the person's spirit before he could awaken, the person was deprived of it.

Also the spirit on occasion left a person voluntarily if it didn't like the body, as for instance, if it smelled badly. When a person's spirit or soul were gone, only the heart was left to keep him alive, and he would succomb easily to the first sickness. For this reason, Atsugewi shamans periodically examined all the people to see if any spirits were missing. When anyone was found lacking his spirit, the shaman had to work to bring it back, sucking it into the person's head. If several spirits were missing at once, it was not easy to get the right spirit back into its own body. They didn't know what would happen if a person got the wrong soul back into his body--- but it wasn't good.

Chapter XXXVI
SHAMANISM AND DOCTORING

Shamans or doctors, more commonly known to modern Americans by the name medicine men, were important in the lives of all Indians but, among ours, probably to the highest degree among the Maidu. Whether we, with our scientific enlightenment today, are after all happier and of greater peace of mind, than the aborigines were or not, is a philosophical consideration beyond the scope of this book. The fact of the matter is that mankind in the past invariably has resorted to the s u p e r n a t u r a l to explain things not understood. Indians are a case in point--- being totally without scientific explanations, mysticism and the supernatural pervaded their whole culture--- their every day activities--- to a point which to us today seems fantastic, yet understandable in a way. If you and I had been in the Indian's place, might not we also have subscribed whole heartedly to these same beliefs with which we would have grown up, and which our loved and trusted elders had taught us in good faith? Shamanism gave to the Indians a feeling of comfort and, shall we say, security? --- a sort of foundation of faith which all men must have for the living of reasonably satisfying lives.

Shamans were men of i n f l u e n c e in the village, with prestige second only to that of the chief. Women shamans were uncommon and usually possessed less potent power. The life of a shaman was precarious because if he failed to effect a high percentage of cures or if he were "proven" responsible for sending pains which caused death to persons, he might be killed--- sometimes even with the advance approval of the chief, and without retaliation by the offending shaman's relatives. When this was done, he was cut into pieces, not for the morbid reasons, the reader might suspect, but for the practical reason that the parts of his body could in this way be disposed of in widely scattered places. Otherwise there was the danger that he might, with the help of his power, be reassembled and again be able to continue his malpractice and to include his murderers among future victims.

There were several kinds of shamans among the local Indians. Each tribe in the Lassen area had the all important Sucking Shaman. Atsugewi and mountain Maidu also had special Bear, Rattlesnake, and Weather Shamans w h i l e only Yana had Singing Shamans in addition.

The power of shamans was much more potent than mere "luck" which came easily to the majority of ordinary mortals in dreams, during puberty ceremonies, and the like. This "luck" was a weak supernatural blessing which was not sought, but came voluntarily and gave the person skill and success in crafts and daily pursuits such as fishing, hunting certain animals or birds, canoe making, et cetera.

It would be impractical in this book to give the complicated and voluminous details of all phases of shamanism as conceived and practiced by each of the four local tribes. The following information has been somewhat generalized in the hope that the reader will get the "feel" of the shaman concept which was essentially the same for all the tribes of the Lassen area.

Power was usually sought by men desiring to be shamans, but all were not successful in such quests. On the other hand shamanistic power came to some voluntarily, and it was dangerous not to accept this power if it came to one. To refuse might cause death. One could tell when one was successful in getting power because one would bleed from the nose or mouth. He would also learn to sing and dance, and would receive instructions and paraphernalia from his guardian spirit.

Shamanistic power could be acquired in a number of ways, not all of which applied to each tribe being considered. A rare means was by inheritance. If an old shaman had power and if this power or guardian spirit liked his son or nephew, it would say "Sometimes I'm going to play with that boy" and so it goes to the boy. At sundown the latter listens to it sing to him and he gets the power. The boy learns about it in the vision and from the old shaman's instructions.

Small portions of yellow hammer or red-shafted quill headbands.

Another infrequent way to gain power was involuntarily when seriously ill, while in a trance, or when dreaming.

The third and usual method of acquiring the shamanistic power was by vision quest. It was a difficult ordeal. This might be undertaken at various times of life, but most commonly at or near puberty. In questing power there was no assurance of success, no matter how sincere a person might be, or how hard he might try. Successful shamans could quest repeatedly for additional powers.

Youths were prepared for questing by being lectured to by fathers or uncles who also pierced their nose septa. Each youth went alone and unclothed into certain portions of the mountains for several days and nights. He slept little and fasted, eating little or nothing at all; all flesh was taboo. The questing usually included swimming in lakes or special pools and placing the nose piercing stick in an underwater niche, and (Yana) securing certain bird feathers. He built a fire, smoking his body over it, and cut himself deliberately. If successful, the power came to him in a trance or faint producing bleeding from the nose or mouth.

The guardian spirit communicated with the novice, appearing in a vision usually. It gave instructions and taught its special ceremonial song. To shamans of some tribes the guardian spirit looked something like a human; to others it looked like a bug or like a small hair. This was the "pain" or poison object and yet was considered to be a guardian spirit at the same time. This is what the novice acquired in becoming a shaman. This pain or guardian spirit could come from any of many sources. It was alive and could talk, and gave the novice certain resultant powers. Most commonly powers were from animals such as coyote, bear, and the like, but also might come from sun, moon, wind, thunder and lightning, eagle, hawk, small birds, reptiles, frog, or oldman spirit.

The novice then acquired what we might call magic feathers. There were several types including the popular salmon colored flicker feathers. Most important, however, was the feather tuft known as kaku among the Atsugewi. This alledgedly was found in finished form and not made. So full of power was the kaku that it could not be kept in a house. It was placed outside securely tied to a willow branch beside a stream or hidden inside a hollow tree trunk. The kaku was able to move by itself so had to be tied down or placed under a rock. When the novice shaman discovered his kaku, the feathers were singing; when he died, blood dripped from its feathers!

Upon his return to the village, the successful seeker stayed out of dwelling houses for a day or two. Among some tribes he was sick for this period. Universally he sweated and swam. Eating habits of the novice shaman varied in different cases, but were always as dictated by the specific instructions given to him by his guardian spirit. Invariably all forms of flesh were shunned. He smoked t o b a c c o and gave his first hunting kill to an old man. During the novice period the new shaman was helped by old shamans at the fireside in the sweat house. He did much dancing, singing, handled hot coals and fire, bled from the mouth, and might fall into a trance.

In contrast to herbalist doctors who gave private treatment, that of shamans was public and usually conducted indoors, preferably in sweat lodges. The shaman needed singing help and the more help and the more persons who attended his doctoring the better. Sucking Shamans were the most i m p o r t a n t and required official assistants. These included one or more interpreters to communicate with the lay helpers or supporters, while the shaman was doctoring, and an outside speaker to help call the shaman's spirits. Doctoring could take from one to three days and nights.

To diagnose the patient's ills the shaman danced about, blowing smoke on him, and s i n g i n g with the help of the audience. The shamans also drank water, sometimes with a tube, from portable stone mortars with spirit power. They often squirted water from their mouths. A whistle was used in some cases and often the supernatural powerful cocoon rattle. Among mountain Maidu herb medicines might be administered to the patient also.

At length the shaman's g u a r d i a n spirit or pain told him the location of the disease object, and then he could see or feel it. Often the shaman learned further from the spirit just who it was who had sent the disease object to plague his patient.

Curing the afflicted was accomplished next by the shaman's sucking this pain or d i s e a s e object out of some portion of the person's body. The evil pain could be any curious small object and this the shaman exhibited to all present. The malignant pain was disposed of in a number of ways. It might be sent back to the owner who sent it, that is, the offending shaman. Or, it might be sent to his children who would be doomed because a shaman could not doctor his own pain. Other times the curing s h a m a n would destroy the disease object by biting it and burning it or dispose of it by taking the pain into his own charmed body.

When a whole community had been affected by a pain sent by an evil shaman, the pain usually hid in the bushes nearby. In such

Maidu shaman
ceremonial neck
pendant knife of
obsidian, nine and
one half inches
long (after Dixon)

a case, the shaman had to be very powerful to get the best of the situation. First he conducted the ceremony of detection of one victim in the usual sweat house manner. Once the shaman found out where the trouble was, he went outdoors with the villagers to help in corraling the offending pain. Frequently only after a lengthy search was he successful in finding the pain and then capturing it. Upon taking it into his body it might be so powerful as to cause him to go into a trance. In this event his assistants had to support him bodily, and had to sing for him, otherwise the shaman might die. Without wishing to appear facetious or disparaging, it can be said that a good shaman had to be an excellent showmen as well.

Sucking Shamans were obligated to accept all cases which they were asked to treat. If they refused any and the afflicted died, then the shamans might be killed themselves by relatives of the persons who succumbed. The thinking was that if a shaman refused a case, he must have had something to do with making the person sick in the first place.

Payment was always made to the shaman. The amount was determinded by the patient's relatives. They would take the offering to the shaman when engaging him, but payment was not made at that time. The shaman looked over the proffered payment and might ask for more or for a different kind of payment. To give himself a foolproof alibi in case of failure to cure, and to increase his prestige if he did cure, he might reply to the effect that "The beads already have the smell of death on them, but I'll see what I can do about it." The payment was placed near the patient during healing treatment and was not actually collected by the shaman if the patient died within a few weeks or months. The shaman's assistants were also paid, but in lesser amounts.

Besides the main function of curing, other good powers of the shamans were the ability to foretell future events, to see what was going on at distant places, and to locate lost or stolen articles. Among certain tribes control of weather was also possible by Sucking Shamans---among others there were special shamans with weather power.

Evil powers of Sucking Shamans could cause illness or death. This was done by talking to the pain and sending it to the victim. The shaman might put it on the end of a willow stick and point it at the person while singing and smoking tobacco. This could go on all night. Transmission of the pain to the intended victim was facilitated by contact, such as sneaking up behind him and touching him, or by putting the disease pain in his food or under his doorstep. The bad pain might also be dispatched by blowing it through a pipe or putting it in the victim's pipe, or by talking to the shaman's own animal spirit, injecting the pain into it and then sending the animal to the victim. This power animal might just take it to the intended person, or it might actually attack and bite him. If the evil pain had been successfully sent, and the intended dire results occurred, the relatives of the victim had a moral right to kill the offending shaman, without fear of retaliation. It seems that the culprit was usually recognized---obviously often mistakenly. It follows that shamans' lives were somewhat precarious, not knowing who was going to find damning evidence against them.

By somewhat the same means as described above shamans could steal a person's spirit or soul, rendering that person liable to quick and sure death from the slightest accident or illness. Shamans could be hired to perform these evil powers.

Singing Shamans were dreamers foretelling the future and telling the living what their dead relatives wanted them to do. The Singing Shaman was always male among mountain Maidu. Our other tribes did not have this specialist, instead such powers were in the repertoire of the Sucking Shaman.

Among Yana and Yahi tribes, apparently, weather doctoring could be done by any shaman, and this was usually the case among Atsugewi. However, mountain Maidu had specialized Weather Shamans. These were men who were capable not only of producing rain, snow, or hail, but also fog and highwinds, or ending any of these.

Rattlesnake Shamans were generally women among Atsugewi and men among mountain Maidu. They could protect people from rattlesnakes or cure bites. The latter was accomplished by sucking which removed snakes and snakes' teeth from the wound.

Bear Shamans did not exist among Yana tribes. Among Atsugewi and mountain Maidu these were not specialists, instead bear power was an additional skill of Sucking Shamans. They were almost always men and pertained not to Black Bear, but only to the California Grizzly.   They wore bear skin, hair, teeth, and claws and simulated the bear's actions in treating patients.   Bear Shamans were called primarily to minister to bear wounded persons from whom they sucked out bear blood and teeth.

Chapter XXXVII
MISCELLANEOUS MAGIC

All tribes of the Lassen region exercised miscellaneous more or less supernatural powers which one might term magic.

Examples were: carrying a turtleshell on one's belt which rendered a person immune to rattlesnake strikes, or, among Maidu the rubbing of the root of *Angelica breweri* on the legs to keep rattlesnakes away. Poisoning of persons could be done by some skilled people (not shamans) by rubbing an unspecified substance on their hands and then touching the victim's body; this could drive him crazy or kill him.

To mountain Maidu the number five was sacred and lucky according to Dixon

Charm stones, usually in pairs were found by many fortunate Indians. They were smooth and rounded and were especially effective if possessing rings or other special markings on them which were actually surface traces of mineral veins. Quartz crystals, rare in this volcanic region, were also highly prized as charm stones. An ideal storage place for charm stones in their special basketry containers was in a rattlesnake "den" where such snakes tended

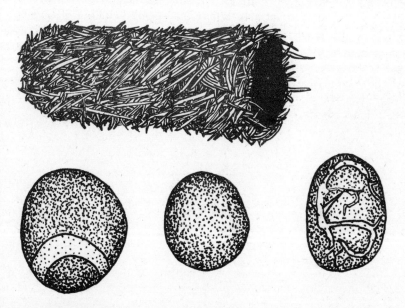

Yana charmstones and a fir twig basket container for such charms.

Atsugewi charmstones

to hibernate in the winter. At any rate charm stones were kept hidden and the owner would secretly rub them on himself to gain good luck in gambling or in other pursuits which involved much in the way of chance.

Prayers for a variety of reasons were offered simply by the individual. It was common practice every few days or so to make token food offerings at mealtime for no specific reason. The bits of food might be thrown to the east or into the fire.

* * * * * * * * * * *

Thus ends this resume of the customs and beliefs of the tribes of the Lassen region --- tribes virtually extinct as such today — tribes which once lived here among the scenic beauties of Lassen Volcanic National Park. We, the descendants of the relentless conquerors of these local Indians, come here now to enjoy ourselves and to refresh our bodies and spirits. As we do this on the lands of the vanquished, we owe them not only a moment of thoughtful reverence, but also whatever kindness and aid we are able to give their descendants.

BIBLIOGRAPHY

Dixon, Roland B.: BASKETRY DESIGNS OF THE INDIANS OF
   NORTHERN CALIFORNIA
   Feb. 12, 1902, Bulletin of the American Museum of Natural
   History, Vol. 17, Part 1
Dixon, Roland B.: MAIDU MYTHS
   June 30, 1902, Bulletin of the American Museum of Natural
   History, Vol. 17, Part 2
Dixon, Roland B.: THE NORTHERN MAIDU
   May 1905, Bulletin of the American Museum of Natural
   History, Vol. 17, Part 3
Garth, Thomas R.: KINSHIP TERMINOLOGY, MARRIAGE PRAC-
   TICES, AND BEHAVIOR TOWARD KIN AMONG THE
   ATSUGEWI
   July 1944, American Anthropologist, Vol. 46, No. 3
Garth, Thomas R.: EMPHASIS ON INDUSTRIOUSNESS AMONG THE
   ATSUGEWI
   Oct. 1945, American Anthropologist, Vol. 47, No. 4
Garth, Thomas R.: ATSUGEWI ETHNOGRAPHY
   Feb. 1953, Anthropological Records, University of Cali-
   fornia, Vol. 14, No. 2
Gifford, E. W. and Klimek, Stanislaw: CULTURE ELEMENT
   DISTRIBUTIONS: II, YANA
   1936, University of California Publications in American
   Archeology and Ethnology, Vol 37, No. 2
Heizer, R. F. and Whipple, M. A.: THE CALIFORNIA INDIANS
   1951, University of California Press
Klimek, Stanislaw: CULTURE ELEMENT DISTRIBUTIONS: I,
   THE STRUCTURE OF THE CALIFORNIA INDIAN CUL-
   TURE
   1935 University of California Publications in American
   Archeology and Ethnology
Kniffen, Fred B.: ACHOMAWI GEOGRAPHY
   1928 University of California Publications in American
   Archeology and Ethnology
Kroeber, A. L.: HANDBOOK OF THE INDIANS OF CALIFORNIA
   1925, Smithsonian Institution, Bureau of American Ethnology,
   Bulletin. No. 78
Kroeber, A. L.: CULTURE ELEMENT DISTRIBUTIONS: XV,
   SALT, DOGS, AND TOBACCO
   Feb. 1941, Anthropological Records, University of Cali-
   fornia, Vol 6, No. 1

Mason, Otis T.: REPORT OF THE NATIONAL MUSEUM
      1902
Merriam, C. Hart: CLASSIFICATION AND DISTRIBUTION OF THE
      PIT RIVER INDIAN TRIBES
      Smithsonian Institute, Vol. 78, No. 3
Pope, Saxton T.: THE MEDICAL HISTORY OF ISHI
      May 15, 1920, University of California Publications in
      American Archeology and Ethnology, Vol. 13, No. 5
Sapir, Edward: THE POSITION OF YANA IN THE HOKAN STOCK
      June 1917: University of California Publications in Ameri-
      can Archeology and Ethnology, Vol. 13, No. 1
Sapir, Edward and Spier, Leslie: NOTES ON THE CULTURE OF
      THE YANA
      Sept. 1943, Anthropological Records, University of Cali-
      fornia, Vol. 3, No. 3
Sauer, Carl O: EARLY RELATIONS OF MAN TO PLANTS
      Jan. 1947, Geographical Review
Vogelin, Ermine W: CULTURE ELEMENT DISTRIBUTIONS: XX,
      NORTHEAST CALIFORNIA
      June 1942, Anthropological Records, University of Cali-
      fornia, Vol. 7, No. 2
Waterman, T. T.: THE YANA INDIANS
      Feb. 1918, University of California Publications in Ameri-
      can Archeology and Ethnology, Vol. 13, No. 2

ASK
THE MAN IN THE
NATIONAL PARK SERVICE UNIFORM

He'll be glad to help you!